The King My Father's Wreck

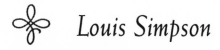 *Louis Simpson*

Story Line Press
1 9 9 5

This publication was made possible thanks in part to the generous
support of the Nicholas Roerich Museum, the Andrew W. Mellon
Foundation, the National Endowment for the Arts, and our individual contributors.

ISBN 0-934257-09-4 cloth
ISBN 0-934257-32-9 paper

Book design by Chiquita Babb

Published by Story Line Press
Three Oaks Farm, Brownsville, OR 97327

Acknowledgments

The chapters were first published in these magazines. "Notes
of the Old Boys' Association": *The Southern Review*. "Moody
Colonials," "The Memorial and the Garden," "Going Back":
The Gettysburg Review. "Waterloo, the Story of an Obsession," "In
Transit," "Lessons of the Body," "The Mouth of Fame," "Love in
the West," "The House of the Stare," "Property and Other
Values," "The Vigil": *The Hudson Review*. "Voices in the Plaza":
Witness. "Baruch" (from "Cleft Houses"): *The Ohio Review*. "A
Window" (originally titled "January"): *Pearl*. "Struga Evenings":
Margin. "Jimmy": *Common Knowledge*.

The poem "Riverside Drive" from *In the Room We Share* is reprinted
by permission of Paragon House. The poem "Working Late" from
Caviare at the Funeral is reprinted by permission of Franklin Watts.

Miriam's Book

In God's intention a meet and happy conversation
is the chiefest and the noblest end of marriage.

John Milton

Weeping again the King my father's wreck,
This music crept by me upon the waters . . .

The Tempest

Contents

4

I

Waterloo, the Story
of an Obsession

I wrote away to England for *Vanity Fair*, enclosing a postal money order. There wasn't a copy at school: the library didn't have one, and it wasn't on the shelves with mildewed books that had been set for examinations. There were copies of *Kenilworth* and *Virginibus Puerisque*, but no *Vanity Fair*.

In the holidays I had seen a movie with George Arliss as the Duke of Wellington, and there were glimpses of the battle of Waterloo, far too brief for my liking. The Duke stood in the stirrups, waved his hat and shouted, "Up, Guards, and at 'em!", whereupon the English soldiers charged and the French ran away. I wanted more of it, and when I came across a reference to Thackeray, saying that in *Vanity Fair* he wrote about the Waterloo campaign, I sent for the book.

It took weeks for my letter to travel by boat to London, and the book to make the voyage back, but it came at last and was delivered to me during evening Prep when we got our mail. I unwrapped the package with an excitement I wish I could recapture. In the days that followed I would take *Vanity Fair* out to the willows and, lying on my elbows, read carefully, aware that this was a classic. I was an avid reader, but for fun—this was the first book I read in the consciousness of the act.

I came to the Duchess of Richmond's ball on the eve of

3

Waterloo. I came to the battle and . . . it wasn't there! I felt a disappointment that, happily, I cannot recapture.

Perhaps the author was meaning to put it in later . . . sometimes they did that . . . in a later chapter one of the characters would look back and remember. But the hope was immediately extinguished. The author had warned, as my heart sank, that he did not "rank among the military novelists." Worse . . . when the decks were cleared for action he would go below "and wait meekly." Now he was saying that for Englishmen and Frenchmen in years to come to continue murdering each other would be carrying out a "Devil's code of honour." There would be no battles in *Vanity Fair*—he disapproved of battles—apparently his middle name, Makepeace, stood for something. I found the point of view incomprehensible. None of the boys at school would have agreed with it, nor the masters who urged us on the football field to play up for the name of the house. How could anyone not enjoy French cavalry charges and British squares wreathed in smoke?

I read on—I had paid for the book out of my pocket money, and as I read I forgot the purpose I had set out with and discovered literature. When I finished *Vanity Fair* I wanted more by the same author—I had fallen under the enchantment of his voice.

It would have to wait till the holidays when I was in Kingston. I would be able to borrow his books at the public library, or perhaps find one on King Street. There was a store that sold cheap editions. Cheap? They were beautiful to me with their red or blue or green jackets and drawings on the inside.

But I didn't have to go to the Kingston library or spend my pocket money. I had a friend named Dennis Anderson. He was my friend during the holidays—there were friends you had at school and friends you saw in the holidays. We went to the same school, in the mountains a hundred miles to the west of Kingston, but I was two years older so that during the term we hardly set eyes on each other. Once at the beginning of term, when we had just got back to school, I was walking on the barbecue with another boy in Form 4A when we encountered Dennis. He spoke to me as though we were still back home. The boy who was with me laughed incredulously—it was unheard-of for a boy in 3A to speak to a 4A boy in this manner. I didn't answer, and Dennis looked abashed as we walked by. But when the holidays started we went swimming together and played ping-pong on his veranda. His house was practically next door—there was only an empty lot between.

Beside these holiday activities we had something else in common: we each had a stepmother. I was fond of mine but never quite at ease—I was afraid of doing something that might offend her. I think that Dennis felt the same. Once when we were playing ping-pong his stepmother spoke to him about something he had done wrong or failed to do. When she went away I saw two tears running down his cheeks.

Our fathers had divorced and remarried . . . they had new wives and had moved to new houses. This was at Bournemouth, to the east of Kingston, an area that was being developed. It was outside the town proper, and I think that my father moved there because he was an outsider. It was not unusual for a married man in Jamaica to have a mistress, but divorce was something else—it was not as respectable in the thirties as it is today.

When he was married to my mother he had a busy social life— they did a lot of entertaining at home. But very few people came to the house at Bournemouth . . . ones he had business with. The "lawn tennis" parties he and my mother gave at "Volyn"—named after the province in Russia she came from—were a thing of the past. By letting his private life be made public he had fallen into disgrace . . . at least for a while. But I can imagine what he would have said if anyone had suggested this. He was a lawyer with a reputation for speaking harshly.

One afternoon I was playing ping-pong with Dennis on his veranda and he was beating me by a point or two as he always did. In swimming too his hand would touch the wall a second before mine. His stepmother Arlene was sitting on the glider doing her toenails. She was an American and dressed like one, wearing shorts around the house. She asked if we'd like some lemonade. I said "No thanks" the first time she asked, as we were taught to do, and "Yes thanks" when she asked again. She went inside to make it.

In a few minutes she called to us. On my way through the drawing room I went over to look at the books. There was a row in green leather with gold lettering. They were all by Thackeray. I couldn't believe my eyes. I had seen them before but not noticed the name. Then it had meant nothing to me.

Arlene saw me gazing. I asked if I could look at one. She said yes, and I took down one of the volumes. The leather was smooth, the paper thick, and the type clear. There were pictures, but not the simple line drawings of the novels with red, blue or green jackets. Those showed people doing something . . . a woman sitting on a chair and a man leaning over to speak to her. A cuirassier on his horse slashing with his saber at a Scotsman in kilts who was reaching up with his bayonet to impale the cuirassier. These pictures were of streets and drawings rooms, marvelously detailed. Of a cathedral. A meadow with cows. There was a sheet of tissue paper over each picture that you lifted to see what lay beneath.

"Would you like to borrow it?" she said.

No one reads Thackeray today—his ideas have not worn well. They were those of an English clubman, far more intelligent than most, but one who has spent his life in one of the professions, and seen much of the world, and has come to the conclusion that all is vanity. After which he orders dinner and smokes a cigar. "Vanity of vanities, saith the Preacher . . . all is vanity. What profit hath a man of all his labour which he taketh under the sun?" Perhaps so, but it is not a thought to sustain you when you have to labor, not for vanity and profit but in order to live.

The world that used to argue over which was the greater writer, Dickens or Thackeray, has opted for Dickens, especially at Christmas. But Thackeray seems to be telling the truth, while

Dickens exaggerates. Dickens's humor is laid on with a shovel and his plots are melodramatic. He does beat Thackeray hands down for sheer entertainment. There's Mr. Micawber and Scrooge, and Magwitch jumping up behind a tombstone to give you a scare. There's Oliver asking for more, and Bill Sikes clubbing Nancy to death and being chased over the rooftops and falling to his death, swinging from a rope. You can't miss the moral in Dickens, while Thackeray may not seem to have one. But Thackeray could tell a story you could believe, and there was something else he could do: evoke the tears of things. Not our tears—you can leave that to Dickens—but the tears of things because we are leaving them behind and only we can speak for them.

But no one reads Thackeray, not even in the university. I said as much to Gordon Ray. I was visiting from California and would be in New York for a few days, and he wanted us to have lunch to discuss some business having to do with Guggenheim fellowships. He was in charge of the program. He was also the biographer of Thackeray, and as soon as I could I brought the conversation around to *Vanity Fair* and an idea I had. I would try it out on Gordon . . . it would be like hearing from Thackeray himself.

I said, "Becky Sharp was Jewish."

Gordon stared and I hastened to explain. *Vanity Fair* was published in 1848. Three years later Thackeray published "Rebecca and Rowena," a burlesque as he called it, of Walter Scott's *Ivanhoe*. "Rebecca and Rowena" tells what happened to Ivanhoe and Rowena after their marriage. The flaxen-haired, blue-eyed, Anglo-Saxon heroine, Rowena, has turned into a pious shrew. Ivanhoe is miserable and yearns for the tender, compassionate Jewess, Rebecca.

Rowena in "Rebecca and Rowena" corresponds to Amelia in *Vanity Fair*. They are both the vapid, butter-wouldn't-melt-in-her-mouth heroine of standard Victorian fiction. By the end of *Vanity Fair*, Dobbin, whose love she has exploited throughout, is already quite disillusioned with Amelia—"Who," the showman asks, "having his desire is satisfied?" In a few years Amelia will have turned into Rowena of "Rebecca and Rowena." And Becky Sharp, whose life runs parallel to Amelia's, and crosses it and diverges, corresponds to Rebecca of "Rebecca and Rowena." As Rebecca is Jewish, so must Becky be.

Of course their characters are entirely different. Becky is "sharp," pushy, on the make, and beyond the pale, as Jews are said to be at the club. Devilish fun, doncher know, but you wouldn't want to tie up with one, not on your life.

A few hundred years ago the English believed that Jews poisoned wells and cut up Christian children in Satanic rituals. By the end of *Vanity Fair*, Becky has become positively witch-like. She has Jos Sedley in thrall. When Dobbin urges him to break off the connection and come away, Jos beseeches him not to say anything about their conversation to Becky: "She'd kill me if she knew it. You don't know what a terrible woman she is." And when Jos dies shortly after, there is a strong suggestion that she has indeed killed him in order to get at the money from the insurance policy he made out in her name. I think that Thackeray is appalled by the life in his puppet, the creation of his own forbidden desires, and is making her repellent so that he can break off his own unfortunate attachment.

What did Gordon make of my idea? I don't know . . . he didn't say, and we went back to discussing Guggenheim business. Scholars have ways of knowing if a man is "sound," whether or not he is a bona fide scholar, and I don't think Gordon thought I was.

Many years later I wrote a letter to the *Times* (London) *Literary Supplement*. They had published an article that said that Thackeray did not write about Jews. I wrote in to say that Becky Sharp was Jewish, pointing out that she anticipated Rebecca in his burlesque of *Ivanhoe*. The editor replied, thanking me for my letter and regretting that they could not publish it.

Kingston had been transformed. The walls were peeling and the roofs were patched with sheets of tin. Houses and gardens had been swallowed up by the town, and people stood on the corners

and stared at you as you drove by. Those who could afford to do
so had retreated into the hills where they lived behind barred
doors and window.

One evening Miriam and I had dinner with Dennis Anderson
and his wife Maura. They lived in one of the safer neighbor-
hoods, but when we drove through the gate two Dobermans rose
to their feet, rattling their chains. A watchman told them to be
quiet, it was OK, and we proceeded to the house.

Dennis was at the door to greet us. It took me a while to make
out, in the face of the confident, socially adept man, the features
of the sensitive boy I had known. He had taken over his father's
export business and expanded it. Maura was an artist . . . the
paintings in the drawing room were hers.

He talked about boys we had been to school with and what had
become of them. The school bully, Weller, was dead. The big,
brawling fellow, Henriquez, who used to box with my brother,
had gone brawling once too often and had his nose bitten off. Jim
Dolan was a contractor . . . he built a big stadium but got in over
his head financially and had to leave the island. He was living in
Miami. Others had done well. Phillips had emigrated to Canada
and made a name for himself in the social sciences. He wrote
books. He had tried reading one, Dennis said, but he couldn't . . .
it was too technical.

Had I been to see the house at Bournemouth where I used to
live? Yes, I said, and had been surprised . . . it was bigger than I
remembered, which was not what people said about going back.
Squatters had taken it over. What I found most surprising was that
a factory had been built in the empty lot between our houses, and
had gone through a cycle of life . . . people had worked there, and
now it was abandoned and falling apart, with cracks in the walls.
It was as though I had closed my eyes for a moment, and opened
them again, and a lifetime had gone by.

It wasn't a factory, he said, but a garage. Anyway our houses,
his father's and mine, were going to be torn down. There were
plans to drive a highway along the shore, connecting with the
road to the airport.

He mentioned people I must know. Did I know So-and-So? No, I said, I didn't. Well, I must know Such-and-Such? I didn't know him either.

He showed me a room with shelves filled with trophies. He had won them by his swimming. and he had taken a swimming team on a world tour. So racing against each other in the pool at Bournemouth had paid off.

His father, Kenneth, had been murdered. One day a man walked into the store on Harbour Street and shot him dead. Kenneth kept a revolver close by but this time he was taken by surprise. He had a mistress and it was said that her husband paid to have it done, but nothing was ever proved. Did I remember his stepmother Arlene? Of course, how could I forget her? I remembered her legs as she sat painting her toenails, and how she let me borrow *The Newcomes*. And *Henry Esmond*, but I bogged down in *Pendennis*. She went back to the States after Kenneth was murdered, and married an architect. She was living in Denver . . . he had a card from her at Christmas.

✤

Like Thackeray I'm at a bit of a loss to know what it adds up to, fact and fiction, things that have happened and things I've read about or seen in movies. Becky Sharp and Amelia and some women I've know . . . a character in Dickens and brawling Henriquez who had his nose bitten off . . . When time has gone by they leave the same impression.

So what is fact and what is fiction? Some people worry a great deal about this. I've known some who threw up their hands in despair and said that nothing was real, only what was in their heads and what they said or wrote. They thought this was real.

Why do you have to choose? Why not just think that everything is real? I've no doubt about the battle of Waterloo—it happened, thousands were there, and for many years afterwards people were talking about it, and some would show you their wounds. Hundreds of books have been written . . . I can recommend

Napoleon and Waterloo, by Major A.F. Becke, R.F.A. (Retired), Hon. M.A. (Oxon.). I wouldn't recommend the French, after all they lost the battle. The biggest whopper is by Victor Hugo: he has a "hollow road" into which their cavalry plunged—that was why they lost. And Stendhal has a description that's a movie by Robbe-Grillet—there are no people, just a landscape and a few figures moving in the distance.

The battle of Waterloo is taking place on June 18, 1815, ten miles south-east of Brussells. It began at 11:30 and is now in the second phase, the attempt to break the British squares with cavalry. Sheer madness!

It begins with a distant rumbling. A line appears on the crest. It thickens and becomes a moving mass. There are lines of horsemen, flashes of helmets and breastplates. The guns in front of the squares fire and the gunners come running back. The ranks open to receive them and close again.

The horsemen are thirty yards away when the order comes to fire. When the smoke clears they are riding between the squares. One will pull his horse's head around and gallop towards a square, but the horse stops . . . it won't do it. The rider brandishes his saber and yells, and is shot out of the saddle. The ground is littered with men in cuirasses lying on their backs like turtles. Others are scuttling away.

There are hurrahs. But they stop. . . . To the front, on the crest of the slope, guns are arriving and being unlimbered. There's the double sound of a gun and the ball buries itself in the mud. Other guns join in . . . the air is full of whistlings and the thud of iron hitting flesh. Something flies by . . . an arm or a leg?

No, just a shadow. I'm lying on my elbows beneath the willows, reading Erckmann-Chatrian. The sound isn't cannon but the *plock* of a bat. The cheers are for our side—they must be piling on runs.

Notes of the Old Boys' Association

"The Munronian" is hoping to receive in future some assistance from the Association and will open its pages readily for contributions of interest to past members of the school.

The Munronian: The Magazine of Munro College.
December 1936.

Sunday, November 27, 1988
5:45 A.M.

I had just had breakfast when the phone rang. It was my brother in Canada. "Mother," he said, "is dying." He had received a call from Italy saying that she wanted to see us and we must come at once.

Miriam called the travel agency. In June when I traveled with her to Italy we flew by Alitalia and missed the connection from Rome to Pisa. We had to wait for six hours in the airport. This time I went by Pan American. During the flight I finished reading *The Romance of the Rose* and made a note of this sentence: "Sorrow . . . is a thing that wounds and profits nothing."

The flight came in on time and I hurried over to Alitalia to see if I could get on the flight for Pisa leaving immediately. I was able to get a seat but the flight was delayed. "The last time I was here,"

I said to an Englishman who was waiting beside me, "I swore I'd never fly Alitalia again." "Well," he said, "it looks as though you've kept your promise."

But the flight did leave. On arriving at Pisa I decided to take a bus into town and find an honest taxi-driver to take me to Viareggio. But a young woman I talked to at the bus stop suggested I take the train. She was studying chemistry at the university and wanted to go to the U.S.A. . . . she had an uncle in San Francisco. She let me know when we came to the railroad station, and half an hour later I was in Viareggio. Then I let my guard down and got into a taxi without asking the fare. That's when they get you, when you're carrying your luggage. He charged L9000 to drive three kilometers from the station to the villa.

Grazia opened the gate. She was surprised to see me . . . I wasn't expected till after five. Then Renato came home with l'Avvocato. He's not only Renato's lawyer, he's a friend and drops by almost every day. He drove us to the hospital. On the way Renato said that he'd told Rosalind I was coming on from Paris . . . I'd been there to give a lecture. I didn't see the reason for making up this story. Then I understood . . . he didn't want to alarm her. My being in Viareggio wouldn't seem so urgent if it were only a stage on a journey.

The hospital is at Forte dei Marmi. We walked through a building, then a garden with hedges, to another building. The hospital is run by the Carmelites whose vocation is caring for the sick. It is well run; the corridors are uncrowded and the patients walking on crutches look at you with friendly curiosity, like residents of a spa looking over the Sunday visitors. I was struck by the contrast to The New York Hospital where Rosalind stayed for three weeks after she had a fall. One day they left her in a corridor, lying on a stretcher, for an hour and a half while she cried and pleaded to be taken back to her room.

Now she was lying with her eyes closed, looking gray and gaunt. A tube ran from her arm to a bottle suspended in mid-air. Renato spoke to her, saying that I had arrived, and she opened her eyes. I told her that Miriam sent her love. She said, "She is a good woman."

She asked for someone by name. The young woman who stays with her went out in the corridor and called one of the nurses. Rosalind grasped the nurse's hand and said, "You understand me." She said that she wanted . . . " What?" the nurse asked. She seemed impatient. Rosalind said something . . . I didn't quite catch the words. The nurse answered brusquely. I didn't think much of her attitude, yet my mother seemed to depend on her. She was looking to her for comfort as though she were a child and this an older woman, a member of the family.

It's like a dream, being back at the villa. I've been studying the bedroom ceiling, fifteen feet high, the chandelier with a candle that is broken and hanging sideways, the high windows with shutters and wooden doors to keep out the cold. The ceiling is decorated with white plaster carved in patterns like lace doilies. The bathroom next door is equally elaborate, with titles rising nearly to the ceiling.

I've been awake since five. The sky is light gray and birds are chirping, cars going by at intervals on Viale Carducci. I'm reading *The Consolation of Philosophy*. For Boethius the only happiness consists in the contemplation of God. Whatever happens to us here is merely an illusion. "Human souls are of necessity more free when they continue in the contemplation of God and less free when they descend to bodies."

But we live in our bodies, and I believe that when Jesus said "The Kingdom of God is within you" it wasn't a figure of speech.

According to Boethius evil is "nothing." He was in prison when he wrote. (He would be tortured and killed in a particularly brutal fashion . . . he was clubbed to death.) This kind of thinking may have helped him to put up with the situation. But we live through our senses if we live at all, and they tell us that evil is real.

"Celestial and divine beings possess clear sighted judgement, uncorrupted will, and the power to effect their desires." Bully for them, but I don't see what celestial beings have to do with us. I believe in a God who suffers or is happy as we suffer or are happy.

When we returned from the hospital there was a telephone call. From Herbert . . . he was at the airport in Pisa. He'd been waiting for two hours and no one had come to pick him up.

Renato had said that Herbert would be arriving on Sunday. I was surprised, for Herbert told me he'd be leaving immediately. Apparently the woman, Sandra Gattai, who takes our calls in English and translates them into Italian for Renato had said "domani," tomorrow, and he heard it as "domenica," Sunday. In any case, here was Herbert, stewing at the airport. Why hadn't he telephoned immediately, Renato wanted to know. A good question . . . he had forgotten his address book, and couldn't obtain the number from Information, for the villa isn't listed under Renato's name but under Barsanti, and there are too many Barsantis in the book. He had obtained the number by telephoning someone in Canada. I told him to take a taxi and gave him the address, and we waited for him to arrive. When he did Renato paid for the taxi.

We had dinner below stairs—it's more convenient than bringing meals up to the dining room on the ground floor. Grazia does the cooking. She also does the housekeeping and answers the door. When there are guests she has a woman in to help her. Grazia is well paid—Renato calls her "Rockefeller" and laughs, but it's no joke. His medical expenses amount to $12,000 a month. Beside the cost of the hospital room Rosalind has private nurses around the clock.

After dinner I sat and talked with Herbert in the study. He talked about Jamaica . . . he'd left in '57 and never wanted to go back. He talked about how badly he'd been treated by his father. I said that I knew . . . I'd seen it. When his father came home from the office he'd go for a walk down to the beach with his wife and their little daughter, Molly. "They never asked me," Herbert says. They treated him like a boarder in the house. In the evening he would go out by himself . . . walk to the tram and go to a movie at the Palace Theatre.

Once he gave a talk at the debating society and someone told his father about it, saying how well he'd done. His father said, "I was surprised. I didn't know you had it in you." He might as well have slapped him in the face.

He says, "I didn't feel a thing when he died."

He talks about the time our father took us to see Uncle Bertie. Bertie was our father's older brother and had been the mayor of Kingston. I recall the visit . . . an old man with a moustache lying sick in bed. I stared at the bed to see where his leg was missing. In the earthquake of 1907 a building fell on Uncle Bertie. He had an artificial leg, a "cork foot." The people had a song about it that they sang at election time:

> Corkfoot Simpson yuh vagabon
> An if ah ketch yuh ah chop off de odder one.

Bertie's landlady came into the room. She was a cheerful, busy woman. With her was a small, colorless man she introduced as her husband. She seemed to have a proprietary interest in Bertie. When we had said goodbye and were driving away our father laughed and said, "Bertie's a rascal." I took this to mean that Uncle Bertie and the landlady were having an illicit affair. Why did he think this was funny? I didn't think that sex was anything to laugh about. I thought about it a lot and would have been ashamed to have anyone know what I was thinking.

This is not what my brother remembers about our visit to Uncle Bertie. He says that when we came home I told him, "It's a lot of nonsense. Why did he want to see us? He never showed any interest in us before." And he tells me how Bertie on his death bed said to our father, "You'll be dead in a year" . . . and he was!

I've heard the story before. Herbert likes stories that seem to have some occult significance. Once when his father took him in the boat to Port Royal he wandered off by himself and came upon the tomb of the man who had been swallowed by an earthquake and cast up again, alive, with a rooster in his hand. On the tomb was the carving of a hand holding a rooster. But the extraordinary thing was that a tree had grown out of the tomb. He was the first, Herbert says, ever to have noticed this.

I've heard this story too, and I don't see what is so significant about a tree growing out of a tomb.

Our talk comes around, as it usually does, to our father's will and how we were swindled out of our inheritance. Before our father died, Herbert says, he called him into the bedroom and told him not to worry, he would be provided for. But the will left all his father's property to his stepmother. Herbert was left the office furniture, with nowhere to put it. His father left him his guns and the *Encyclopedia Britannica*. What was he to do with the guns? Start a revolution? There's no doubt Amy forged the will. She could imitate Aston Simpson's signature to perfection.

Not only have I heard my brother's stories . . . I was present at the scenes he describes. But he appears to have forgotten and speaks as though he were an only child. When I remind him that I was there he seems surprised. He considers the idea, almost with disbelief.

He says again that he didn't feel anything when his father died and they had a funeral. He felt about it as I felt about the visit to Uncle Bertie . . . it was a lot of nonsense. Our father had wanted to be buried at sea because of his boat, "The Seahawk," in which he used to go around the harbor. But they ignored his wishes and had a big funeral.

Sunday morning.
Herbert says, "There were lawn tennis parties at Volyn before your time." But I was there . . . I remember the tennis parties. I've even written about them.

In Jamaica, he tells me, people sent their children away to

boarding school at the age of nine. I can't help interrupting: "How old do you think I was when I went to Munro?"

He stares at me . . . "I have no idea." I tell him . . . I was nine.

Life at Munro was brutal. People don't believe it when he tells them that the masters beat the boys with canes and the bigger boys beat the small. There was one boy who was "oblivious to pain." He was given a licking, then he turned around and asked the master, "Have you finished?" This continued until the master was too tired to lift his arm. They saw the boy's back in the shower afterwards . . . it was crisscrossed with red welts.

He tells me that if you looked in the Sixth Form window the big boys called you in and made you run the gauntlet, kicking you from the far wall and out through the door. I'm the one who was kicked, and he's telling me about it!

Many of the boys he went to school with were "shot down in the war." I express some disbelief . . . I can't see Jamaicans rushing to join the colors.

No . . . H.B. did and was killed over France. I remember him . . . we called him "Scratchy." He got the name, Herbert says, because he had a line to speak in the school play, and when he delivered it he stood scratching his arse. Now I seem to remember the incident and how the audience howled with laughter. Scratchy had a friendly, foolish way of smiling, and fair hair that kept flopping in his eyes when he boxed. He wanted to learn how to box and followed my brother around—Herbert was an avid boxer. I can see Scratchy pushing out a straight left and throwing his head back to get the hair out of his eyes. His chin stuck out, inviting a punch. He hadn't the slightest talent for boxing.

I imagine Scratchy in a bomber . . . maybe one of those big Wellingtons, and what it must have been like when the plane caught fire and started to go down.

Herbert talks about S., the prototypical English boy who was good at everything . . . cricket, football, boxing, running, gym. He was "head boy" and top of the school in his studies. In later years S. became a barrister, then nothing more was heard of him.

In this too, I think, S. was typical. There was a certain kind of boy who was brilliant in school and did nothing much afterwards. Perhaps they knew fame too soon and had nothing left to wish for, or the qualities that enable you to shine where there are rules are not qualities that succeed in life.

He asks if I have ever heard from my friend, Peter. Yes, I did get a letter from him once. He was working for an airline in Brazil, shipping freight. But the letter came at a bad time . . . I was going through a bad patch in my life and didn't have the energy to write, not even to Peter. Years later I wrote to him but received no answer.

He was sensitive, Herbert says . . . his feelings might have been hurt.

He coached Peter at the inter-school boxing competition that was held in Kingston. Peter was up against a big fellow. Before the fight started he told Peter, "Just box him. Don't throw the right." In the second round he told him to go for the stomach. To illustrate he hits his palm with his fist. When the third round came he said, "Now throw the right." Peter did and the fellow was out for two minutes. It frightened Peter . . . he thought he'd killed him. He never boxed again . . . hung up the gloves.

He keeps returning to his father and to Amy, the stepmother who intrigued against him. Once when they were out in the boat he talked back to his father and Amy turned to him and said, "See what I mean?" It is due to her, he thinks, that he has had so much trouble in his relations with women. I say that the trouble may have started earlier when our mother left Jamaica. He thinks this over and seems to fall in with the idea. He remarks that even before she left he saw very little of her . . . she was playing golf at the Liguanea Club. He was brought up by the servants.

He remembers how it was when his father took him bird-shooting. There were two black boys, one at each side, who watched for the birds and called "Mark left!", "Mark right!"

Life could have been wonderful when he was growing up . . . his father had so many varied interests.

He is telling me an incident that occurred when he was in the boat with his father. They saw hats, pieces of clothing, and toys floating on the water. An excursion boat had capsized, drowning twenty people. He tells me the story without the slightest awareness that I was there—and of course he wouldn't know that I've written about it.

❖

We drove to the hospital with Renato. He insists on driving though he has a cataract and his vision is poor. He drove slowly, drifting over the median line. Once or twice I thought we were going to be hit by an oncoming car.

Rosalind appeared to be comatose . . . she'd had a bad night. We tried talking to her but she hardly responded. I read the label on the bottle attached by a tube to her arm. It was a five per cent solution of glucose.

She became fully awake and complained of nausea. She was suffering . . . wanted to be moved to a new position. Her head hurt. . . . The nurse moved her and rearranged the pillows.

Why does she cling to life? I think because she's never had enough. From stories she told I gather that she never felt really loved. When she was seven her father went away to America. The factory that he owned burned down—people said that the fire was caused by Gypsies who camped nearby—and there was no other way he could make a living. There were seven children. So he went to America to earn good wages and send money to Russia.

The mother and her daughters scraped along somehow. There was one boy, the youngest child. The grandmother was the real head of the family; she made knishes filled with kasha, hard-boiled eggs and, in the winter, goose fat fried into small chunks that were eaten with bread. She sold these out of the house.

Grandmother had been married twice. The first time was to a man who kept a shop selling leather. One day a cossack came into the shop with a hide he wanted to sell. He bargained with the shop-keeper, then suddenly he picked up a hammer that was lying on the counter and struck him with it in the head, killing him instantly.

I like these old stories of family life in Russia.

Rosalind slept in the same room with her older sister, Lisa, and Lisa's husband. The room was divided by a curtain. In the night she would hear them whispering. And there were rats in the walls . . . sometimes they ran across the floor. She slept on three chairs pushed together. The chairs slid apart while she slept and she would fall to the floor. She pushed them together, picked up the bedclothes, and climbed back.

The father who had gone to America died suddenly. Then her mother took three of the children—beside her own she now had Lisa's to care for—and went to America, leaving Rosalind behind with the two youngest. They were to follow later.

During this time, when she was living with relatives, Rosalind must have felt that she had been abandoned. She has always been alone. This is why she clings to life, waiting for a happiness that was promised, listening to Lisa and Lisa's husband whispering behind the curtain.

Renato drove us back from the hospital. He couldn't see clearly and drifted to the left, in the path of oncoming traffic. With the sun in his eyes he couldn't see whether the lights were red or green. I would tell him "To the right!" I would say "rosso" or "verde." It was like the W.C. Fields movie where the blind man comes into the drugstore, feeling about with his cane and breaking glass. But being driven by a man who is almost blind isn't funny.

I invited my brother to dinner at the Ristorante Montecatini. We walked on the street that runs parallel to the sea for two miles. At 7 P.M. some shops were still open and we looked in the windows.

We talked about our mother. The gray doll propped on pillows and being fed intravenously, drop by drop, bears no resemblance to her. Rosalind has always been active and strong-willed. She did as she liked. She was headstrong . . . and, I remark, she would order people about if they let her.

Herbert said that in Caracas she accused his daughter of

stealing her clothes. What would a fifteen-year-old girl want with the clothes of a middle-aged woman? Once an American millionaire came to visit and she accused his daughter of stealing her fountain pen.

As I write these notes I see a reason for her accusations . . . her feeling that she missed out on the good things of life when she was growing up. She was cheated of her girlhood. She didn't have anything when she was a girl, so why should they? Why should a girl have a millionaire for a father? They have stolen something from her . . . her clothes . . . her fountain pen.

I am pleased with myself for having thought of this and I tell Miriam. She says, "Did they steal the things?" I reply that my brother doesn't think they did, and tell her what he said about a girl not wanting the clothes of a middle-aged woman. He could be wrong, she says . . . Rosalind always has nice things. So much for my theory! It could possibly be true . . . that's all that can be said for it.

I tell Herbert about Rosalind's quarrel with D. when we stayed at the Villa Rosalind. She patronized D. . . . "It's an estate, my dear. You wouldn't know what that is." Herbert says, "I suppose D. didn't say anything but let the pressure build up." This is true, and I remember when the boiler blew . . . D. shouting at Rosalind and pulling Annie away from her. They didn't speak to each other again for twenty years, not till they met at my son's wedding.

We talked about our parents' marriage. Herbert says that they were completely unsuited to each other. Our father was suited to his mistress, Amy, whom he married later, and Rosalind is suited to Renato who has a cheerful disposition and is devoted to her.

At the Montecatini we help ourselves to *antipasti* . . . not as varied as they were in June when I came with Miriam. We order *branzino*, a local fish, with a side order of spinach. I order a bottle of wine.

My brother talks about pranks he played as a boy . . . in order, he says, to get some attention. His father had a rolltop desk. It fascinated him . . . in one of the drawers he came upon a medal from the Freemasons. His father was proud of it . . . it had a round piece of gold in the center. Herbert extracted the gold piece with his teeth . . . he has always had strong teeth, he tells me. He carried the piece of gold around with him, and one day he put it under his plate at the dinner table. The maid removed the plate suddenly . . . Herbert tried to retrieve the gold piece but too late, his father had seen it. "What's that?" he asked. When he saw what it was he was dumbfounded. He didn't flog Herbert on this occasion . . . he was too astonished. He sent him to his room to dine on bread and water.

The waiter tells me that our bill has been taken care of, charged to Barsanti. I tell him to bring it anyway . . . Renato has enough to pay for without paying for our dinner. The bill comes to L100,000. The grilled *branzino* was good, and it was a good bottle of *chianti*, but still!

We retrace our steps. The shops have closed . . . everyone's at dinner. My brother continues talking about his father. Rosalind once showed him a letter his father had written. She'd written to Aston from Canada, after the divorce, urging him to pay more attention to Herbert. He wrote back saying, "Do you think I'm going to waste my time on a boy?"

Why, Herbert says, did she show him the letter? It had hurt him to see it.

One day he took his father's revolver, the big one, out of the rolltop desk. I remember it . . . the Webley service revolver. He took it to the kitchen and pointed it at the cook. His father gave him a flogging for this. He had a rubber belt that he used to flog him with.

He says that when his father came home the first thing he'd say was, "What's he done today?"

I begin to laugh and Herbert is pleased with the effect his stories are having. I tell him that I'm losing sympathy and beginning to see our father's point of view. I imagine him coming home from his office or the law court and having to deal with Herbert. He is the best lawyer on the island and a sportsman. He can fix

anything in his "carpenter's shop." But he comes home to Misrule
. . . a son who is unpredictable and incorrigible, no matter how
often he's flogged.

One day he put crayons in the cover of a shoe polish can and
melted them on the stove. He had discovered that if you melted
crayons the colors ran together, producing a pretty, marbled
effect. He placed the hot cover on his desk to cool. The governess,
a woman he hated, came into the room and, seeing the cover, said
"What's this?" and picked it up. The metal was still hot . . . .

I am laughing so that tears run down my cheeks. My brother's
stories aren't so funny, but we're both laughing . . . in Italy, so
many years later, far from the place where we were born. Our
father has brought us together after all. Who could have predicted
this? I imagine him listening and not understanding, a puzzled
look on his face.

Later in the evening, reading in bed, I come upon this passage
in Boethius:

> Whenever something is done for some purpose, and for certain
> reasons something other than what was intended happens, it is
> called chance. For example, if someone began to dig the ground
> in order to cultivate a field and found a cache of buried gold. This
> is believed to have happened fortuitously, but it does not happen
> as a result of nothing; it has its own causes, the unexpected con-
> junction of which have clearly effected the chance event.

Mother lies with her eyes closed and teeth clenched. Her plate of
semolino hasn't been touched. The nurse, Vincenza, asks her, "Are
you angry with me?" Mother doesn't answer, and for the three
hours of our visit she doesn't say a word. Her eyes open now and
then, the lids open slightly, then she dozes off. She snores and
utters a series of high-pitched cries that indicate she's in pain.

We have an interview with the doctor. She says that the situation is "brutta," ugly. Mother isn't cooperating, she is refusing to
take nourishment and there's no way to make her take it . . . since
the recent "edema" her heart couldn't stand the strain. I say that

it's as if she wants to die, and the doctor nods to indicate that this is so. I ask if it's because my brother and I are here . . . she may have been holding out till we arrived. The doctor smiles at the idea as if to say it's absurd, but I'm not convinced.

I walk to the end of the corridor. A glass door looks out on mountains, snow-capped peaks. In the foreground umbrella pines.

I think about sanatoriums in the Alps . . . *The Magic Mountain* and *Tender Is the Night*. It seems that everything I do brings to mind something I've read. I used to think this was something to be ashamed of . . . there's a tradition in the States that puts down any kind of learning. Writers are supposed to be naive, and the characters in American fiction don't think about books.

But in Chaucer they do. I'm looking forward to teaching Chaucer in the spring.

November 29

6:45 A.M. The anxieties and inconveniences of travel . . . and the unreliability of travel agents.

At the Alitalia counter in Pisa I'm told there's no record of a reservation. Fortunately there's room on the flight. Am I sure that I have a reservation from Rome to New York?

I made both reservations at a travel agency in Viareggio. The woman made them over the phone and I paid her L10,000. I hope she wasn't talking to a non-existent person at the other end of the line.

In flight to Rome . . . the people and things you see when you travel! An old woman sitting across the aisle takes a newspaper from the stewardess. She tears out a page and tears the page in half. She puts one half on the other and lays them on the vacant seat beside her. She tears out another page, tears it in half, and puts the torn halves with the others. This continues until the whole newspaper has been torn in half pages and these have been placed in a pile.

She takes one of the half pages and looks it over. She takes another . . . and tears out an item of news. She puts this in her handbag and pushes the discarded piece of paper under the armrest. Now there's a pile of crumpled newspaper.

She turns her head and meets my stare. Her eyes are dead . . . like knobs of rubber.

Who said that? Faulkner, speaking of Popeye. I read it many years ago in the room I shared with my brother. Certain words make a lasting impression.

Moody Colonials

When I was nine I was taken from my home in Kingston to a boarding school in the country. Munro was a hundred miles to the west, a considerable distance in those days. You drove across the island for hours. The last stretch was a road that wound with hairpin turns up a mountain. You passed through a gate and saw a line of willows and the red roofs of the school.

Boys were running about and shouting. When it began to be dark a bell rang and everyone went to the dining room where you were told to sit at one of the long tables. The headmaster rapped with a spoon and everyone stood while he said, "For what we are about to receive, may the Lord make us truly thankful." You sat down and the master at the head of your table heaped gobbets of pork from a tureen onto the plates. They were passed down the line and one came to you. There was a bowl of spinach, and a bowl of rice that had been cooked until it was a sticky mass. For dessert, a kind of watery custard. You could hardly eat . . . the food was very different from what you ate at home.

After dinner you were told to go to one of the classrooms. I was in the Second Form, the lowest in the school. A master came into the room and gave us a book and some sheets of writing paper. The book was Latin . . . the words arranged in columns. He said that we must learn all the words on the first page by heart. He wrote numbers on the board . . . multiplication and long-division sums. Latin and arithmetic were our "prep" for the evening. I set about doing the sums, dipping the nib in an unspillable inkpot.

After what seemed a long time the bell rang and everyone went to the chapel. A master stood at the front of the chapel and said, "Let us pray," and we kneeled on a cushion while he said a prayer. Then we sang from a hymn book:

> He who would valiant be
> Gainst all disaster,
> Let him in constancy
> Follow the master . . .

When the hymn came to an end we sat down and the master read from the Bible and said, "Here endeth the lesson." There was another prayer, then we filed out of the chapel and went to the dormitories. I was in C Dormitory. There were twenty beds, with a table at each end of the dormitory on which stood white-enameled basins and pitchers of water. Under each bed there was a white chamber pot. I undressed and got into bed. The sheets were cold and the blanket rough. Then it was "Lights out." I lay listening to the wind shake the roof. You weren't allowed to talk after lights out, not that I felt like talking or knew anyone to talk to. I was thinking of what the next day might bring.

Munro College was said to be the best school on the island, "the Eton of Jamaica," but there was a cultural lag between the colony and the Mother Country, and the best school in Jamaica was no better than a second-rate English school, the kind George Orwell would describe in "Such, Such Were the Joys." The boys were at the mercy of the masters, whose onsets of bad temper found a vent in caning a boy or maybe half-a-dozen. You could be waked out of a sound sleep in the middle of the night to be caned because someone had been making a noise. There was a considerable amount of bullying of small boys by the big boys, and of course no one told. My cousin Douglas who went to Jamaica College, a day school in Kingston, and came home to his family every night, was far happier than I.

It was a strange idea of bringing up children, to send them away from home and let them be treated harshly, but this was done by the best families in England, and so it must be right for us. The model was the same throughout the British Empire. I had a pen pal in New Zealand with whom I traded stamps, and his letters about his school were such as I might have written. The boys' magazines that came from England, the *Gem* and *Magnet*, and the red *Chums* annual that my father gave me every Christmas, presented a version of what public school life should be. There was a boy named Tom Merry or Dick Cherry to whom everyone, even the masters, deferred. He was good at games and his ethics were above reproach. There was a boy whose father was a lord—he wore a monocle and said, "Bai Jove!" There was a Canadian boy, and a "dusky" boy from India who was good at cricket. There was a fat boy, Billy Bunter, who was always scheming to obtain pork pies and other goodies. He would be caught doing something he shouldn't, and be given six on the backside by a prefect, one of the bigger boys who, under the masters, were empowered to run the school. Billy Bunter yelled "Leggo!" and "Yaroo!" as the fives bat, whatever that was, landed on his bottom.

There were villains too in these stories, boys who didn't play games and behaved in a furtive manner. We supposed this meant that they smoked. At Munro some boys would have a "hut" in the woods, actually just a space walled around with leaves and branches, where they smoked. If you were caught smoking you would receive a severe caning.

Public schools are said to have been hotbeds of vice. Some of the older boys at Munro bragged about having had sexual intercourse, and there was some sexual experimentation between boys, and jokes were made about it. This may have been vice, but a great deal of innocence was going on most of the time.

Games were very important. The sportsmaster was an Englishman who had played football professionally on one of the English teams. He spoke with a cockney accent, he couldn't pronounce his aitches, and he taught, of all things, English grammar and composition. Every afternoon we lined up on the barbecue. The sportsmaster would call out two boys to captain the teams, and they would call out names until there were eleven to a side. He would call out another two boys, and they would make up two more teams. Any illusions you might have about your playing were dispelled as names were being called. It was like being on the slave block . . . fine if you were a good player, but if you were not you might stand there while other boys were called until you stood among the very last. At the side of the barbecue were a few boys who had a note from the school nurse excusing them from games that day, perhaps for a boil or a cold. When the last of the players had run off to the fields, the sportsmaster walked over and looked at the excuses with undisguised contempt.

We played cricket and football; we ran around the track, high-jumped, and pole-vaulted; we did gymnastics, and we boxed. At every boxing session the sportsmaster would say, "Simpson Two and Fox," I suppose because we were well matched and put on a good show. Charlie would hit me in the head and I would hit him in the stomach. Sometimes the whole school ran across the countryside following a trail of bits of paper, and came straggling back to the school. This was the only time you were allowed to leave the grounds—at any other time it was a grave dereliction. If you were caught out-of-bounds you would be caned by the headmaster himself. He was a stout man with small piggish eyes and a yellow moustache who taught Latin to the upper forms with a cane in his hand. We lived in fear of the day when he would be teaching us. For a very serious offense you would be given a licking by the headmaster in front of the assembled school.

Some years after leaving Jamaica I came to know an Englishman who had been a prisoner of the Japanese during the Second World War. The Japanese commandant had the amusing idea of beheading a prisoner now and then in front of the camp. This caused one Englishman to have nightmares during which he would cry out in terror. One night while he was having a particularly noisy dream, one man said to another, "What's wrong with him anyway?" "He thinks," the other replied, "that he's back at

Winchester." In telling this story, substitute the name of the public school of your choice.

I suppose there was a good side to our Spartan life. I have been able to put up with a fair amount of physical discomfort, I have not been too particular about my food, and I don't have an exaggerated idea of my importance. You could hardly think of yourself as a little tin god when the toilets were open and in plain view of anyone walking by. If you were outstanding in some subjects, as I was in English and French, you might be poor in others, as I was in math and science, and our masters did not hesitate to hold a backward scholar up to ridicule. There was none of your stuff-and-nonsense about damaging a young person's self-esteem— ours was damaged repeatedly. It was a lot better, we thought, than the damage that could be done to one's person by six on the backside, or being made to write five hundred times, in neat handwriting, "I am a lazy and ignorant boy."

There is a possible benefit of a public school education that I discovered in a novel by V. S. Naipaul. I think the best ideas are found in fiction, or perhaps I should say that ideas are best expressed in fiction. In Naipaul's *Guerillas* the writer Roche says that he is not usually afraid, and attributes this to his having been educated at a British school. He says, "It's the way I am. It probably has to do with the school I went to. I suppose if you accept authority and believe in the rules, you aren't afraid of any particular individual."

If you accept authority, yes . . . and if everyone else accepts it. But suppose the authority were removed? Then it could be a free-for-all, and the devil take the hindmost. This is what happened in some colonies when the authority of Whitehall was removed and the people had to fend for themselves. In some places there were riots and massacres. Order was restored by having a single party or a military leader.

"We are just," the English said. "With us every man is equal before the law, whatever his color or race. Think what it would be like to be governed by those without the law."

As I have said, ideas are best expressed in fiction, and the best explanation I know of the colonial situation is in *The Tempest*. The native, Caliban, says to the European, Prospero,

> This island's mine, by Sycorax my mother,
> Which thou tak'st from me.

Caliban admits that being civilized was, at first, a happy experience.

> When thou cam'st first
> Thou strok'st me and made much of me, wouldst give me
> Water with berries in't, and teach me how
> To name the bigger light, and how the less,
> That burn by day and night . . .

"And then," Caliban says, "I loved thee." Prospero and his daughter Miranda had missionary zeal. Prospero let Caliban share his cell, and Miranda taught him the use of language.

> When thou didst not, savage,
> Know thine own meaning, but wouldst gabble like
> A thing most brutish, I endowed thy purposes
> With words that made them known.

But there came a great change that reduced Caliban from a petted creature to a mere slave, a fetcher of wood, punished by Prospero with cramps if he disobeyed.

Why did Prospero change? Because Caliban attempted to violate Miranda, to use Prospero's term for what may have been a clumsy attempt at seduction. From that time forward, instead of being stroked Caliban has been whipped. And it is not just Caliban the individual monster who has been condemned, but his whole race. "Thy vile race," Miranda says,

> Though thou didst learn, had that in't which good natures
> Could not abide to be with.

Caliban is base by nature and will remain so—no amount of learning will make him a European gentleman.

We know that all Europeans were not bent on enslaving the natives they came across on their voyages of exploration—some believed they were bringing light to darkness and treated the natives kindly. But even with the best of these there was the assumption that the native was inferior. Otherwise, what need to raise him up? In any case, the native was made to feel inferior. Think what it must have been like to receive Miranda's teaching. The more Caliban learned, the more he realized how ignorant he was and that he was predestined to be inferior to his European master and mistress, separated from them by a net that was invisible yet as strong as steel . . . everything that made the European superior to the savage.

At first Caliban thought of Prospero as a father. Why should he not? Why else would Prospero be treating him so kindly? But then Caliban came to understand that however well he behaved Prospero would never regard him as an equal, and however hard he studied he could never be Miranda's husband. The language he had been learning said that all men were equal in the sight of God; it spoke of justice and truth and beauty. It drew pictures in the air of palaces and towers, and people in fine clothes riding in coaches. But this world was not for him. The European might educate the native but was not about to admit him to the circle of power.

Miranda did not regard Caliban as a man; he was a savage, hardly more than a thing in her eyes. So he attempted to possess her and so even the scales. Now Caliban found himself worse off than he was before Prospero and Miranda came. Then he was ignorant, but he was king of the island. Now he was a slave. "You taught me language," he tells Miranda, "and my profit on't / Is, I know how to curse."

This fable goes to the heart of the colonial situation. In Jamaica when I was growing up you were taught to think like the English. You learned English history and literature, and that you owed everything to England, and owed her your loyalty in return. But you were not English—to be English you had have been born in England. So there was a sense of inferiority built into the colonial psyche.

In Jamaica race was not the barrier that it was in South Africa or Mississippi. One year the head boy at my school was a perfectly English type, straight out of the *Gem* or *Magnet*. The next year the head boy was colored. In Jamaica a colored man of ability could rise to the top. There were places where he might not be welcome —he might not be able to play tennis at the Liguanea Club or go swimming at Bournemouth, but if he had any pride he wouldn't want to.

Race was not the most important thing about a person—class was, what you did and how much money you had. Your standing in the community. In this the colony was very much like the Mother Country. Snobbery was, and still is, the besetting vice of the English. But though snobbery is a vice it is rarely fatal.

My father was a successful lawyer, so I was sent to "the Eton of Jamaica" and taught to think of myself as English. I became quite a snob. The more I liked Shakespeare, the less able I was to find poetry in my surroundings, and the more uncouth the native speech sounded to my ears. The more I read English history, the more I thought that our own was a puny thing, and even that had been made by Englishmen: English soldiers and sailors, English planters, and English authors.

We did not study Jamaican history or geography, but I do recall once being made to draw a map of Jamaica. How empty it seemed! Instead of wheat fields and apple orchards, bananas and sugar cane. The railroad that ran from Kingston into the hills, puffing and hooting at a snail's pace, could not compare with the "Royal Scot" and "Flying Scotsman" speeding from London to the north. Why draw a map of Jamaica? If we were clever enough, one day we would be living in England.

Our hygiene text explained that a family in the English midlands could have an adequate diet "by ringing the changes on pease and beans." It told us how to economize on coal during the winter months in Manchester and Leeds. It was hard not to think that the tropics were unreal and our lives were unreal. Real life was taking place in England.

To be a colonial was to be always apologizing for a deficiency, a falling short of the ideal. But the time had come when people were no longer willing to feel this way. The Marxist says, "First the stomach, then philosophy," but in the twentieth century we have seen repeatedly that people are willing to put their feelings before their stomachs. The colonial system was breaking up everywhere in the thirties because people were no longer willing to be treated like children and wanted to be their own masters for better or worse.

The point was made in the movie about Gandhi a few years ago. It is after the incident at Amritsar where British soldiers shot down hundreds of Indians who had assembled peaceably. The outcry is such that the British governor has called a meeting with Gandhi to discuss what is to be done. One of the Englishmen present remarks that, under Britain, India has been governed well. The actor who plays Gandhi answers softly: he asks the speaker to consider whether there is any people that would not prefer to govern itself badly than be governed well by another.

The changes that were occurring in the world outside were also occurring in our school. In the late thirties Munro was transformed by a new headmaster, A. G. Fraser. He held discussions with the Sixth Form . . . we discussed a book by Aldous Huxley that dealt with such matters as nonviolent resistance, the revolutionary technique Gandhi was using. This was a far cry from the old headmaster who taught Latin with a cane in his hand. My last years in the upper forms were filled with the excitement of learning. With Mr. Wiehen I read Racine and Molière, with H. J. Andrews I read Shakespeare. And I was reading all sorts of literature on my own: I discovered T. S. Eliot and D. H. Lawrence. The education I received in those years was as good as any that was being given in England. This was demonstrated: our examination answers were sent to England to be graded.

There was a catch: it was an English, not Jamaican, education. I don't want to suggest that I was aware of this at the time, or that many people were aware of the real reason for their dissatisfaction.

They thought it was the machinery of their government, being governed from London—I don't think they would have said that studying in English schools had given them a feeling of cultural inferiority. They wouldn't have said that the ability of West Indians to think and write like West Indians had been neglected. On the contrary, middleclass Jamaicans were proud of their English education—they thought the language of the lower class positively funny. As for writing and the arts . . . wasn't Shakespeare far better than anything a West Indian had written or might write for the next three hundred years? But I ask you to consider: is there an author who would not prefer to write something fairly good of his own than read a masterpiece written by another?

This is what Caliban discovered. When people from a more advanced civilization undertake to teach you, or perhaps it is only a more advanced technology, little by little your belief in yourself is taken away. It is insidious, for in many ways your teachers are doing you good, giving you language, law, medicine, and a railroad. But the sense that the island is yours has been taken away. This may not matter urgently to a lawyer, doctor, or engineer, though it must matter to them too in the long run. But it matters immediately to a writer. You won't die of a feeling of cultural inferiority, but you may fall silent. Your thoughts, by being adapted to the language of others, may cease to be your own and become theirs.

I discovered this point of view during a vacation in Kingston when I met other young men who were writers but were not in awe of English literature—they were writing poems and stories set in Jamaica and using Jamaican words and phrases. They weren't trying to write like Englishmen and failing, they were writing like themselves and therefore succeeding.

Living in Kingston, they were aware of the movement for independence that was getting underway. People were demanding better wages and working conditions, but they wanted more. "How now?" Prospero says to Ariel. "Moody? / What is't thou canst demand?" And Ariel replies, "My liberty."

There were strikes and riots. The British troops marched out to confront the rioters, shots were fired, and men were killed. The young writers I met were not throwing stones, but they had seen that life for Jamaicans could not be what it was for the English. They were tired of apologizing for their way of life. They would write about the things they knew, as Wordsworth had written about the Lake District, and Thomas Hardy about Dorsetshire, and Lawrence about the Midlands. These Jamaicans had learned their English lessons well . . . they had learned how to be themselves.

They were encouraged by a few men and women of an older generation: the editor of *Public Opinion*, who published their poems, articles, and stories, and Edna Manley who invited writers and artists to her house. It must have been there that I met M. G. Smith, George Campbell, and H. D. Carberry.

Smith was an intellectual. His training had been in science—in an article or story he might use an algebraic equation to make a point. In his poems he wrestled with thoughts about the universe and used metaphors drawn from science.

> Must I gravitate
> In one ascetic segment? And fraction
> Each year's arc?

I believe that Smith became an anthropologist . . . like other men and women with a gift for literature he found science more rewarding. I have always envied such people their knowledge of science. At the same time I have wondered how they could give up writing poems and stories, for I know of nothing more exciting or, in the long run, more useful.

George Campbell wrote poems that were like flowers—they were feelings purely distilled. They shone like stars and sparkled like dew.

> Daylight like a fine fan spread from my hands
> Daylight like scarlet poinsettia

> Daylight like yellow cassia flowers
> Daylight like clean water
> Daylight like green cacti
> Daylight like sea sparkling with white horses . . .

H.D. ("Dossie") Carberry wrote both poems and stories, and became my friend. We wanted to write . . . poetry, fiction, essays, anything.

Public Opinion accepted three of my poems and a short story. One of the poems, "Desire," described the landscape at Munro, Top Rock and the willows lining the drive. The description is sexually suggestive.

> Willows on the highland gesture together
> With prudent hands to roaring weather,
> The scandalized rock
> Sends strength to each tether
> And holds down its frock.

The story, "In Love and Puberty," is written in the first person—I have been reading William Saroyan. Like Saroyan's fiction this is not so much a story as a series of impressions—as my narrator, Ronald Callot, says, "there is no fixed perspective." And there is no plot: he takes a bus downtown to the library, swims at the Myrtle Bank Hotel, and takes a bus back. But though he has no fixed perspective, he reflects—he is resisting the blandishments of middleclass life that he sees as about to possess him.

> Soon there will be the polishing of car fenders, the drawing-room floor, the furniture—the caressing of possessions . . . but not yet.

He thinks of the girl he is in love with and exclaims against "the beautiful logic of probability" that keeps her out of his reach. He thinks about the need of Jamaicans to find their own identity as a people.

What shall be created out of a century of perversion? A pendent, incomplete people. The crying ghosts of a lost race, the half ashamed.

But when he smiles at some children playing in the gutter they don't smile back.

They stand silently, without speaking or moving, their eyes indifferent to alien blow or kiss.

The story concludes with a cry: "Oh Christ, that it is as it should be!"—a protest against the inexorable, unfeeling logic of existence . . . the way things are.

My cousin Douglas tells me that Norman Manley liked this story, but my Aunt May had a different opinion: she read it and sniffed. There was quite a bit of heavy breathing in my narrator's yearning for the young woman, and Aunt May was of the old Presbyterian persuasion that did not speak of such matters.

May was my father's sister. She lived with another sister, Edith, who had married the Postmaster General, Reginald Fletcher. There were four children of the marriage. I remember their family as distinctly my own, perhaps because it was such a contrast. My father and mother were divorced when I was a child, and my mother was compelled to leave the island. In the time between my mother's leaving and my father's marrying again, I stayed with the Fletchers. They were a happy family. In my memory it is afternoon in the South Camp Road. My aunts are sitting on the veranda rocking and fanning themselves. A tram goes by, squealing on the rails. A breeze springs up from the sea, rustling leaves of eucalyptus and lignum vitae. My cousin Sybil brings the box of board games onto the veranda, and she and I play Snakes-and-Ladders. It was Sybil who started me writing when I was small . . . she was writing a story and encouraged me to try.

There is a thumping sound in the background . . . Douglas hitting a tennis ball against the garage. He is good at games as well as being a good scholar.

On Saturday everyone gets in the car and we drive to the sea.

There is a line of cabins. Piles have been driven in the sea floor with wire netting to protect against sharks and barracudas. Waves are rolling in and breaking, and we splash in the sea. Coconut trees along the shore are swaying and dipping in a stiff breeze.

But Sunday is different . . . a Scottish Sabbath. You have to be quiet and not go running about.

When my father remarried, my brother and I went to live with him at Bournemouth, on the harbor. I was away at school except for the vacations, but my brother left school and was articled to my father and lived at home. Herbert had a miserable time. He didn't get along with his stepmother, and he was failing his law exams. Now and then our mother came to the island to see us for a short time. Her visits were clouded by the thought that she would be leaving again.

My father died when I was sixteen. His will made no provision for sending me to a university. He would probably not have wanted me to go anyway: he thought that young men who went to a university came to no good . . . in spite of his having Norman Manley for a friend. Manley had studied at Oxford. But my father was sure that English university life was a round of dissipation. Or did he think it made young men conceited and gave them extravagant ideas? In any case, he left no money that would take me to England. My only chance of going was to win a scholarship, and that was very unlikely—the scholarships almost always went to the science boys.

So when my mother wrote and asked if I would like to visit her in New York, I didn't hesitate. I got on the mail-van at Munro that took you to the train at Balaclava. In Kingston I packed a few belongings in a suitcase, and two books, *Pride and Prejudice* and Bradley's *Oxford Lectures on Poetry*. I had borrowed the Bradley from my English teacher, H. J. Andrews. It was given him as a prize at school. I never got around to returning his book. It stood on a shelf staring reproachfully at me.

✤

F. O. Matthiessen, in his book on Theodore Dreiser, says that Dreiser's outlook was colonial. Dreiser grew up in small towns in Indiana and German was spoken in the home. At the turn of the century, the centers of culture were on the Eastern seaboard—for a young writer, New York. Matthiessen remarks that those who grow up in a province or colony are in the habit of thinking of the center of power as being distant from themselves.

I know that I have a tendency to think this way . . . to think that power and authority are outside myself—someone else is taking care of things. This makes you feel secure—at the same time it makes for resentment. It is an old colonial way of thinking and it doesn't work in the modern world, if it ever really did.

I am not saying that this way of thinking holds true of every ex-colonial. Norman Manley, who became the Premier of Jamaica, and Edna Manley who did so much to encourage Jamaican art and culture, consulted their own feelings—they did not look outside. But I think there may be many who have felt as I. It is one thing to declare independence, another to overcome the habits of the past and the influence of powerful nations, cultures that are older or overwhelmingly stronger than one's own.

It is a legacy of colonialism to think that if we do our lessons everything will come out right. It is easier to accept someone else's way of thinking than to discover what we ourselves feel and want.

My father, like other self-made men, did not feel a need to question the system in which he had done so well. He believed in work. If you applied yourself in your profession, everything else— the relations of man and wife, of parent and child—would fall into place. He went to work every morning, and hard work it was . . . defending an East Indian who was being sued for non-payment of a debt, defending a dock worker brought up on a charge of assault. He worked late into the night preparing a case while his wife, my stepmother, typed a legal document. My father's house was an extension of his law office.

There had been a time when he read stories of travel and adventure. The old books with gilt covers stood on the shelves of his study. If you opened them there were drawings of exotic beasts . . . a jaguar crouched on top of a capital letter T, waiting to pounce on the explorer. A python wound around the letter I, waiting for the unwary marmoset. There were books by Rudyard Kipling . . . ballads about British soldiers in India . . . a horrendous story about a man who was trapped in a pit where the dead were thrown. There were best-sellers of the nineteen-twenties: *The Sheik, The Green Hat.* . . . Or had these belonged to my mother?

One book was certainly hers, *The Victor Book of the Opera* with its pictures of opera houses in Milan, Paris, and San Francisco . . . Scotti, Caruso, Galli-Curci. The men wore tights and were armed with swords, the women were garnished with jewels. They leaned on a balcony looking dreamily into the distance.

If my father had once read and enjoyed such books and listened to music, he no longer did. In the late afternoon he drove home from his office in Tower Street, or from Spanish Town where he had been arguing a case. He came up the steps with a briefcase full of law books in his hand. If *John O'London's Weekly* had arrived that day he would hand it to me.

He sits in his chair on the veranda reading *The Daily Gleaner* and smoking a cigar. A sea breeze rustles the vine, and the moon is beginning to climb above the harbor, on her journey to America across the sea.

2

In Transit

Every Friday night members of the family gathered at my grandmother's apartment in Brooklyn: my mother's younger sisters, Ruth and Annette, her niece Dorothy and brother Joe. My mother was usually absent; she was traveling, demonstrating cosmetics for Helena Rubinstein . . . at first in the States, then in Central and South America.

When I was growing up in Jamaica my mother did not mention her Jewish background. She wanted to put behind her the poverty of her early years in Russia and her life as a working girl in New York, sewing tucks in shirts. She admired the English who were at the top of the social heap in Jamaica, their fine way of speaking and good manners. She learned to serve tea at four o'clock in the English fashion, and played golf at the Liguanea Club.

There were Jews in Jamaica. The first book ever published by a Jamaican, a translation of the psalms of David, was by a Portuguese Jew, Daniel Israel Lopez Laguna. In the second half of the sixteenth century when Jews were driven out of Spain and Portugal, they were glad to find a haven in the West Indies where they were not persecuted. As time went by they prospered, but they did not want to draw attention to themselves and their religion. My Presbyterian aunts, who had a little to say about everything, did not speak of Jews. They did, however, talk about Catholics. It might have been only the day before yesterday that Cromwell seized the island from the Spanish and made it a British colony. Whenever a chicken or turkey was served at the table Aunt May was sure to point out the Pope's nose.

At school I attended Anglican services in the chapel twice a day. I was appointed to read the lessons from the pulpit, the first boy at Munro to do so. It was an experiment—the lesson was always read by a master—and I passed with flying colors. The words and rhythms of the Old Testament as well as the New were imprinted on my mind, but I did not make a connection between people I read about in Scripture and anyone living today. I had never, of my own knowledge, seen a Jew.

I had a best friend at Munro with whom I walked up and down on the barbecue every evening talking about trains and boxing. His name was Peter Lopez. But for his Jamaican accent Peter might have been taken for an English boy. It was not until years later, reading an article about Jews in the West Indies, that I learned that Lopez was a common name among Sephardic Jews. I don't think Peter was any more aware of this than I.

When I came to New York I discovered that my mother was a Jew and therefore, according to Jewish law, so was I. My grandmother spoke English with a Yiddish accent. She was very religious. I can see her lighting the candles on Friday night, bringing her hands to her breast and praying in silence. A few years ago she had made a trip back to Russia, bringing clothing and money that she distributed, enabling some young people to marry.

But her daughters had shed their religion in mid-Atlantic. They had given up their Jewish traditions and been assimilated, but only on the most superficial level. Ruth was the receptionist at a beauty salon, Annette ran a theatrical agency, Dorothy was somebody's secretary on Wall Street, and my mother sold cosmetics. They were happy to dine in a restaurant and go to a Broadway show—they seemed to want nothing more. I don't think I ever heard them discuss a book or article they had read.

and there was no man in the family with whom I might talk about ideas that were important to me. My mother's brother Joe was a pharmacist and worked in a drugstore a few blocks above Times Square. Joe was a good soul but his life was circumscribed by the pills and eyebrow tweezers he sold and the wife his mother had picked for him to marry.

There was one who was different, Molly, Dorothy's sister. She was married and lived on Long Island. When I took the train to Woodmere I saw something of a life that was familiar: houses, trees, and sky. I went to the beach with Molly and her children, Freddy and Lee. Since coming to New York I had felt disembodied, but as I swam out to sea and looked back at the land I was myself once more.

I was a Jew according to the law, but that was all. I had nothing in common with bland, assimilated Jews who cared nothing for the word. On the other hand I had nothing in common with the men I saw walking on Kingston Avenue, my grandmother's people with their beards and fish-white complexions, their black hats and overcoats, speaking a foreign tongue.

My mother was renting an apartment in Manhattan on 53rd Street, just west of Fifth Avenue, next to the Museum of Modern Art. As she was usually away on business, Ruth and Dorothy lived there too. When my mother returned from one of her trips she would take me to dinner in a restaurant and give me advice.

One piece of her advice I have never forgotten. I was about to enter college, and she told me not to let anyone know that I came from Jamaica—I was to say that I came from England. She did not give a reason but it was obvious: if I said I was Jamaican people would think I was colored. It did not seem to occur to her that this advice might make me think there was something I should be ashamed of—which it did. For years I felt uneasy about having been born in Jamaica. It did not occur to my mother that it was wrong to tell me to lie.

Fortunately all my training had been in the other direction: I grew up thinking that to lie was a sin . . . unforgivable. I did not take her advice—and it made me dislike her. I thought that in her business, cosmetics, she was continually lying about the products she sold, saying they would make women beautiful when, in fact, the face creams and "skin nourishers" were only grease. I thought she was always pretending to be something other than she was, and all her ideas were wrong.

In the early 1940's she was traveling far afield in Latin America. Her talk that had been punctuated with the word "dollars," so that I had to resist the impulse to put my hands over my ears, was now punctuated with the word "bolivars." I was happy to return to my room in the dormitory at Columbia and the reality of poems and stories.

❖

There were two courses all Columbia College students had to take in their first year, Humanities and Contemporary Civilization. Humanities was a course in great books ranging from Homer to Kafka. Contemporary Civilization took care of everything else, a ragbag of political economy, sociology, and psychology. I preferred the great books and was fascinated by each in turn. One week I would be immersed in Thucydides, another in the plays of Sophocles. The course, however, did not include poetry except as an adjunct to drama. This was typical of the tastes of the faculty at Columbia. With the exception of Mark Van Doren, who was a poet, they had very little respect for poetry. What they liked was an idea that could be argued about. The teacher I had in Humanities four times a week, Lionel Trilling, typified this attitude.

Trilling had considerable charm and was held in awe by his students. Not only was he a professor, he had connections downtown, publishing articles in *Partisan Review*. He was the author of a biography of Matthew Arnold and short stories that had been anthologized. I thought his classes fascinating though I was often disappointed because he did not address the aspect of a work that excited me. On his part he had no high opinion of my contributions to the class discussions. Once he asked us to name a present-day writer of comedy. I put up my hand and said "P. G. Wodehouse." "Oh Mr. Simpson," he said sadly, and gazed out the window at a tree with his luminous eyes. It would be some years before *Partisan Review* decided that Wodehouse was a major author.

At the end of the first semester Trilling gave me a middling grade. Two of my classmates went to see him and complain on my behalf—they said I was one of the best students in the class. At least, this is what a man told me long after. The story may be true though I find it hard to believe. At the end of the second semester, however, Trilling did give me an A.

The course made a great difference . . . how great I would discover when, as a teacher, I rubbed elbows with colleagues who knew nothing beyond their field, *The Faerie Queene* or the Victorian novel. And it has given me a skeptical view of contemporary authors, the kind who air their opinions on television. Can they really think they are so important? Or is it just publicity?

There is a nineteenth-century painting of Napoleon on the deck of the "Bellerophon," being transported to exile on St. Helena. He is wearing the cocked hat he seems never to have taken off and his hands are clasped behind his back as he stares at the sea, lost in his thoughts. Some British naval officers are watching him covertly at a distance. This was how people looked at Trilling in the corridor of Hamilton Hall when he stepped out of his office . . . a mixture of awe and apprehension. For they were aware of his power to do harm. If he thought an instructor was not "the Columbia type" the young man would find himself looking for a job. On the other hand, if he liked you he might give you a book to review or recommend you on graduation for a job in a publishing house.

Van Doren was the opposite of Trilling. The core of his character was a love of literature. His teaching was spontaneous—he told you what came into his head, and there was a great deal in his head. Teaching such as this cannot be methodized—it depends, as T. S. Eliot said criticism must, on being very intelligent. It is in disrepute at the present time in universities for not many students are very intelligent and literature makes demands on them they cannot meet, the first being an understanding and love of poetry. It is far easier to adopt and cleave to the sayings of a Derrida, a de Man, a Stanley Fish.

> Blind mouths! that scarce themselves know how to hold
> A sheep-hook, or have learnt aught else the least
> That to the faithful herdsman's art belongs!
> What recks it them? What need they? They are sped;
> And when they list, their lean and flashy songs
> Grate on their scrannel pipes of wretched straw:
> The hungry sheep look up, and are not fed,
> But swoln with wind and the rank mist they draw,
> Rot inwardly, and foul contagion spread . . .

During the week my courses kept me busy and I had friends to talk to. My best friend was Ted Hoffman: he read my poems and gave me the encouragement I needed. But weekends, when the students went home to their families, could be lonely, and the vacations at Christmas and Easter were times of desolation. I went for long walks on Riverside Drive and took my meals in cafeterias. I would go to a movie by myself, perhaps at the nearby Thalia that showed avant-garde movies like *The Blood of a Poet* or the Stanley Theater at Times Square that featured movies from the Soviet Union.

As a schoolboy I had been taken with English poets of the Left, Auden, Spender, and their circle. I had written for *Public Opinion*. At Columbia I told my friends I was a socialist; in dormitory discussions I would talk authoritatively about Marx and the Soviet Union. Now the Soviet Union was at war with Germany—a colossal struggle taking place in the snow. Movies at the Stanley, where I got my information, showed Russians as a nation of freedom-fighters and lovers of democracy.

I took the subway back to Columbia and my room in John Jay, twelve floors above the street. It was beginning to snow. Lights blurred and the flakes built layers on the windowsills across the way. Traffic noises were hushed. A foghorn boomed in the distance.

I picked up Yeats's *Collected Poems* and in a few minutes forgot that I had been feeling lonely and there was a war.

Riverside Drive

I have been staring at a sentence
for fifteen minutes. The mind
was not made for social science.

I take my overcoat and go.

Night has fallen on Riverside Drive . . .
the sign for Spry shining
across the Hudson: "Spry for Frying ****
for Baking."

I am thinking of Rilke
and "Who if I cried would hear me
among the angelic orders?"

It seems that we are here to say
names like "Spry" and "Riverside Drive" . . .
to carry the names of places
and things with us, into the night

glimmering with stars and constellations.

Lessons of the Body

> He vaguely desired to walk around and around the
> body and stare; the impulse of the living to try to
> read in dead eyes the answer to the Question.
>
> *The Red Badge of Courage*

I enlisted in the army and was sent to a tank regiment at
Camp Bowie in Texas. I was the loader and radio operator. I sat
in the turret surrounded by shells as the tank went jolting and tilting at alarming angles. I would have preferred to be in the infantry
where my fate would lie in my own hands and feet.

From Bowie the regiment moved to Fort Hood. Then I was
selected for the Army Specialized Training Program and sent to
the University of Louisiana at Baton Rouge to study engineering,
for which I had no aptitude. The program was suddenly terminated and I was sent to the 75th Infantry Division at Fort Leonard
Wood, Missouri. There, standing over a machine gun in the
woods, with snow falling and my feet freezing, I had my wish.
Years later, on the subway in New York, I saw a man named Pucci
who had been in the tank with me. He told me the regiment had
gone to Europe . . . the tank had been hit, the driver killed and he
himself wounded.

I was taken out of the division and shipped to Northern Ireland as a replacement. And there I joined the 101st Airborne Division stationed in England. The 101st was an outfit of parachute and glider infantry you volunteered for. I don't recall volunteering, but there I was, at Reading, in the 327th Glider Infantry. Perhaps in a moment of recklessness I put up my hand. Northern Ireland was dismal . . . it rained continually . . . I may have volunteered out of desperation, hoping for something better.

The regiment was supposed to go into combat in gliders but on D-Day, the sixth of June, we waded ashore on Utah Beach. We were lucky . . . by the time we landed there was no opposition on the beach itself. The battleships firing their 16-inch guns, and the P-47s and Spitfires plunging toward the ground and firing rockets and machine guns, must have taken care of any Germans in the immediate vicinity. We marched inland, passing fields and *bocages*, the hedgerows that would soon be notorious. They were thick and tough, each hedgerow a line of defense where the enemy could lie concealed.

The files parted and the men in front stepped around an object lying in the road. A man was lying face down. He was dressed in the steel helmet, green fatigues, pack, and paratrooper boots that we wore, and he was dead. This was fascinating—we would have liked to walk around the body and stare.

We came upon other bodies lying at the side of the road. These were German. They lay with their rifles in a litter of equipment . . . gas masks, mess kits, shovels. They wore mustard-colored camouflage and raincoats that looked like capes. It didn't take long for every man in G Company to know that we were facing parachute infantry, the best they had. Information travels fast down the line.

It was a cool, fresh day in June. Shells from the battleships lying offshore went fluttering over. A German tank was standing in the road. It had burned, and one of the crew had climbed halfway out the hatch before he was engulfed in flames. Now he was a substance, black and red, that flowed down the side of the tank. It looked like burned rubber.

The order came to fall out and we sat and rested, leaning back on our packs. The First Sergeant motioned me over . . . I was the Captain's runner, carrying his messages. I was to tell the lieutenant of the lead platoon to take the fork to the right at the next crossroads.

I went up the road at the double, passing the men spread along the banks. They called to me . . . "What's up?" I shook my head to show that I was as much in the dark as they, at the same time making a gesture with my hand to reassure them . . . it couldn't be important. I gave the lieutenant the message and made my way back to Headquarters Section.

An order was coming over the radio. We were to stay where we were and dig in. The company arranged itself among the hedgerows by platoons and squads and you were alone. When night fell you opened the K-ration. You mixed the powdered coffee with water in your mug. The K-ration box would burn. You made a fire at the bottom of your foxhole and ate the meat and the two fortified biscuits. You smoked one of the cigarettes. Then you shoved down in your sleeping bag. An hour later a plane came over. It circled with a throbbing sound, German, and dropped a bomb that whistled and shook the ground.

Something was moving about in the darkness to our front. There were rifle shots. When morning came dead cows lay among the hedgerows, their legs sticking up.

We resumed our advance, marching at combat interval, riflemen out in front and on the flanks. We came to an open field crossed by a railroad embankment. Machine guns were firing from the other side, bullets passing overhead. We lay in the shelter of the embankment.

Bullets were sweeping to and fro directly above us. In a few minutes the order would come to go over the embankment. We were like infantry in the Great War waiting to go over the top. I had read about trench warfare and looked at photographs . . . a line of men with helmets and rifles looking up at the camera. In a few minutes many of them would be dead. There were photographs of bodies that had lain in No Man's Land for weeks and months . . . in one case, years. A skeleton clothed in rags.

The order did not come. Two of our planes swooped over, Thunderbolts, and fired rockets at the ground we could not see, on the other side. They made several passes, firing their machine guns. Then the order came to move out, and we climbed the embankment. The guns had stopped firing, and when we came to the end of the field there was the usual litter of equipment, and the bodies of the ones who had not been lucky, flies already settling on their open eyes and mouths.

It may have been the next day that we came to a wooded strip of land with water on each side. We were walking in the usual files with a squad strung out in front when guns began firing at us. I knew the sound very well. The German machine gun fired faster than ours, and their submachine gun, the Schmeisser, positively purred. I dropped face down. Six inches above my head a wicked, white gash appeared in a tree trunk. There was an explosion . . . another. The ground trembled. The explosions walked down the strip of earth on which we were lying, footsteps of an approaching giant. I felt a blow in my back, a very light blow, on the shoulder blade. The giant walked by.

About ten feet away a voice was calling "Mamma mia!" It called over and over. It would stop calling for a moment, then resume.

The footsteps were coming back. Again they passed by me, showering my back with twigs and leaves. Bullets hummed and ricocheted among the trees. I reached my right arm down my side and, without raising my body from the ground, unbuttoned the flap of the entrenching tool carrier and eased out the tool. I brought it in front of me without raising my arm, and moved the blade to the open position, and screwed the collar so that it held the blade fixed, and began scraping the earth to make a depression.

The shells continued walking among us, choosing whom to kill, whom to wound, whom to pass by. They were mortar shells and made no sound as they fell through the air. I felt a trickle of blood running down my back . . . it was a blessing. "Until the next time," the giant said as he walked by. All the time I lay there the voice near me was calling "Mamma mia!" Finally it stopped.

Shells were coming over from behind us, going to the German machine gunners and mortar crews. We were no longer being fired on. We stood up and went forward again, along the strip of trees, beside the water. There were houses at the end and the beginning of a town.

There were two brothers, twins, in G Company. One was the man who lay near me calling for his mother. He died there, and his brother went through the rest of the war with an air of sad devotion. One day in Holland when the company was in the same fix, but this time it was German .88's that had us lying on our faces, shells coming straight at you like rifle bullets, flat and scream-ing, with only a moment between the sound of the gun and the explosion, I carried shells to the mortar the dead man's brother served. I remember the look he gave me when I kneeled and let down the cloverleafs into his hands. The look said "Thanks." That look meant more to me than any praise I have had since.

A few years after the war I was living in Paris as a student, though little studenting I or my friends did, for we found the pro-fessors at the university ridiculous—all they seemed to care about was your pronouncing French correctly, they cared nothing for ideas. We spent our time in the cafés between St. Germain and Boul' Mich, talking about writers we admired.

I had still not recovered from the war. It was no trouble to see bodies lying about in my room, one with an arm held rigidly in the air, another with a knee drawn up. There was a German officer who kept reappearing on the furniture. I had first seen him lying on a mattress outside a house in Holland—he had been carried out of the house and left on the mattress to die in comfort. Since then he had swollen so that his belly was bursting his trousers and his arms and legs extended stiffly like balloons. Now he had got off the mattress somehow and would turn up in my room at odd times, perching on a chair and looking at me. I offered him a cigarette which he refused, producing a packet of small black cigars from a pocket. Turkish, he said, which he preferred.

One night I dreamed that I was walking with other shadowy figures along what seemed to be the bank of a canal, when bullets slashed the trees and shells were falling. I woke and wrote out the dream, and as I wrote remembered . . . it wasn't a dream, it had actually happened. For one of the symptoms of the mental disorder that came after the war was amnesia . . . there were bright patches with darkness all around. Now this scene came back clearly.

I wrote it as a poem. I had been reading Heine's ballads, and the poem took the form of a ballad. As it was a poem, not just a memory, I was free to invent.

> Tell me, Master-Sergeant,
> The way to turn and shoot.
> But the Sergeant's silent
> That taught me how to do it.
>
> O Captain, show us quickly
> Our place upon the map.
> But the Captain's sickly
> And taking a long nap.
>
> Lieutenant, what's my duty,
> My place in the platoon?
> He too's a sleeping beauty,
> Charmed by that strange tune.
>
> Carentan O Carentan
> Before we met with you
> We never yet had lost a man
> Or known what death could do.

The poem is well known, in so far as poetry can be known in our time, but I once read an article in which the writer said that it was only a "tour de force." He found fault with what he called the worst stanza.

> Everything's all right, Mother,
> Everyone gets the same
> At one time or another.
> It's all in the game.

When I wrote that stanza I was not thinking of myself but the man who died near me calling on his mother. It is true . . . this is a simple stanza, but these were simple men. They were not literary critics. Most of the hard and dangerous work of the world is done by such men. During the war I learned to respect them and have done so ever since.

I have earned my living by teaching in universities. The people around me, with a few exceptions, could not understand the basis of my thought . . . that words to me were pale in comparison with experience, mattered only in so far as they transmitted experience. In recent years, with the spread of what is called theory, I have come to dislike some of my colleagues very much, those who have taken their text from Saussure and who teach that there is no direct connection between words and life, only between one word and another, one "sign" and another.

There is another kind of person who fills me with dislike. One evening at dinner in New York a woman told me that she thought it terrible that I, a poet, had been in the war. She had a son who was about to enter Columbia and he would never take up arms.

No, I thought, some other man will do his fighting for him.

In the Forest

The first regiment of the 101st Airborne Division reached Bastogne by the first hours of December 19th. By nightfall that same day the entire division with all four regiments had unloaded from their borrowed trucks and deployed for defense in and around the town.

Danny S. Parker, *Battle of the Bulge*

I remember the ride in open trucks from Rheims to Bastogne, and digging a foxhole among the trees. While we were digging it began to snow. We covered our foxholes with branches and took turns standing guard, four hours on and four off. You could hear the guns and see fires burning where the fighting was taking place. When morning came a heavy fog hung over the forest.

To read about the fighting at Bastogne is to remember how little those who were there knew of what was happening. Our officers must have known where the regiment was situated, but they didn't tell us—all that we needed to know was the ground in our immediate vicinity. I was a runner and carried messages through the woods from G Company to Battalion. The First sergeant would give me a message—verbally, so there was no chance of its falling into the hands of the Germans. I repeated the message back to him, to show that I had it right. Then I set off, trudging through the trees. The snow lay thick on the ground and branches. The Ardennes were shrouded in fog so that the sky seemed to be reaching down to the treetops. No sun could penetrate the overcast.

I arrived at the house that was occupied by Battalion, delivered my message to a sergeant, and stood at the stove to warm my hands and feet. I was given the answer and trudged back to the company.

It occurred to me when I was carrying messages that I might run into the Germans. The thought didn't bother me, for I didn't think it would happen. I believe this to be true of many who have been in combat: they went through it with a sense of unreality and the conviction that nothing would happen to them. This would not, however, prevent their dreaming about it afterwards, perhaps for years, reliving in dreams the confrontations that never happened.

The men on the line passed along whatever information they had. We knew that the division was surrounded, and we were told that the Germans were killing prisoners. At Malmédy they killed eighty who had surrendered. Army Headquarters passed the news to the troops in order to stiffen their resolve.

The hours seemed interminable. You stood in your foxhole, stamping your feet, or lay down in your sleeping bag. We were living on K-rations and going hungry. The only diversion was making a pile of twigs in the foxhole, with strips of waxed paper torn from the K-ration box, and lighting a fire. Over this you heated a can of water from your canteen, and mixed the powdered coffee and milk and sugar.

Our feet were freezing. Our boots were unlined, and though the rubber overshoes kept them dry these made our feet sweat. Then the moisture would freeze. We had not been trained to take care of our feet in such conditions, and many of the men developed "trench foot." That was what it was called in the First World War, but as we were not in trenches I preferred to call mine "frozen feet."

On December 22nd the 101st received an ultimatum, surrender or else. People in New York and Wichita Falls heard about it . . . we didn't. I read about it weeks later in a hospital bed in Paris, with my feet hoisted in a sling, the treatment then given for trench foot (years later it was decided that the thing to do was to keep your feet warm—which was what you wanted in the first place). I read that the German commander Von Lüttwitz, who sent the ultimatum, spoke of "one German artillery corps and six heavy A. A. battalions" that were ready to annihilate the troops encircled at Bastogne. To which General McAuliffe, who had the good fortune to be temporarily in command at Bastogne, our regular general being absent, answered "Nuts!"

In the days that followed we were shelled heavily. This, and being cold, is what I remember most clearly about Bastogne. Shelling is what ground troops experience most frequently in combat—this is their war. The first time you are shelled it takes a while for what is happening to register. Up to now, combat has been an abstraction, explained to you in training and on maneuvers. Now you realize that someone is trying to kill you—it seems a most unreasonable thing for anyone to want to do. While your mind is making its adjustments, your body is on a course of its own, contracting when a shell comes in. When you have been shelled a few times, your body is fine-tuned: it can tell if a shell is going to land fifty yards away, or twenty, or practically on top of you. But though you become experienced you never become accustomed to shelling, for experience doesn't help—the next shell could kill you as easily as the first. Troops don't necessarily become more efficient with experience—they may become more cautious. The happy medium—happy, that is, from the commanding general's point of view—would be for the troops to have had some experience of combat, but not too much.

The men who were wounded had to be taken back to Bastogne as soon as possible. If they were left exposed to the cold they would die. On December 23 the overcast cleared. American planes were over Bastogne for the first time, dropping food and ammunition and medical supplies. Fighter-bombers attacked the German positions . . . the flames of their vehicles could be seen around the perimeter. But the temperature fell to fifteen degrees and the shelling was intense.

On Christmas Eve a messenger came to the company and announced that there would be a religious service at Bastogne for men who wanted to go. I seized the opportunity to see people and hear human voices, and joined the group who were making their way to Bastogne. There were prayers and the Chaplain gave a brief talk. He said that we were far from home and missing our dear ones and our Christmas dinners with turkey and all the trimmings. Some of us might be wondering why we were here. We were defending our way of life, so that we could go back to it and pick up where we'd left off.

This, trite and uninspired as it may seem, was true. A later generation, after the war in Vietnam, would not be able to understand the feelings of the men who fought in the Second World War. It was not easy for them to put their feelings in words—the patriotic speeches that were delivered at the end of movies did not speak for them. But they were as strongly motivated as was needed if the occasion should arise. In the Ardennes, in the winter of 1944, they destroyed the German army.

On Christmas Day the Germans attacked in the sector held by our regiment, south-west of Bastogne. Volksgrenadiers accompanied by tanks broke through the line of riflemen for nearly a mile before they were stopped. In this attack the Germans lost eighteen tanks and two hundred men, killed or captured.

On one of my journeys through the forest I came to a road. A Sherman tank was standing on the road, one of the tanks of the 10th Armored who were with us at Bastogne. The hatch was open and the tank commander was in the turret, looking down the road. A German tank was burning. He looked at me as I walked by, and turned again to watch the road.

I can see him still, like a man at ease in the saddle, as I go on my way, looking back.

The Mouth of Fame

What a thing to be in the mouth of fame.

Keats

I was renting an apartment in the East Fifties, a fairly large room with a kitchen along one side. Nick Carraway says that life is much more successfully looked at from a single window, but mine faced a brick wall.

According to the terms of the divorce, my very young son, Matthew, could visit on weekends. We would go to Central Park and the Zoo or the Museum of Natural History, perhaps a movie. I played with him, made dinner, and put him to bed. Then I worked at my writing. A few years before when I was living in France I published a book of poems. It received two or three encouraging reviews, but I had published it at my own expense and you weren't an author until you had a publisher. My poems were appearing in magazines and I was putting another book together.

I worked as an associate editor for a publishing house. I got there at nine, pulled out the bottom desk drawer, put my feet up, and read a manuscript. When I had read enough to know what I thought I would type a brief description and my opinion, and start the pile that would go to the editor-in-chief, J. B., at the end of the day. He would either reject the manuscript or pass it on to a second reader. Besides myself there were Michael Gallagher and Frieda Bunsen. When we disagreed, J. B. would make the final decision.

Sometimes he let one of us edit a manuscript that had been accepted for publication. Or confer with an author about needed revisions. I cut 300 pages out of a historical novel and wrote chapters in the author's style to join the hemorrhaging parts. The author, a Frenchman, wouldn't mind so long as he received his royalties. I rewrote the English sentences of a German who had designed rockets for Hitler and was now designing them for us.

J. B. was more than a boss, he was a friend. At the office he was too busy to exchange more than a few words with you. He was conferring with authors and agents, with the Vice-President in Charge of Sales or the Office Manager. But you were invited to his house on Saturday, and sometimes to sleep over. He lived out on Long Island, and I looked forward to these excursions, a welcome change from my brick wall. The train unrolled houses half-hidden among leaves, green fields, and glimpses of the sea. I was approaching the real thing, Fitzgerald's "green breast of the New World."

At the office J. B. wore a business suit, some dark color . . . on the Island it was loafers and jeans. He had two daughters by his second marriage, Jennifer and Julia, fourteen and twelve, and a boy, Henry, by his first. His present wife, Milly, was on friendly terms with Henry's mother, and Henry got on well with the girls. There'd be a game of softball with the neighbors' children or we'd go picnicking on the beach.

In the afternoon people would drop by . . . the lawyer who lived next door, a woman "in theater," an author or two, some strange fish among them. There was a Hungarian who was writing a novel based on his experiences as a refugee during World War II. J. B. had given him a contract and I had read the novel . . . it was deadly dull. He smoked cigarettes with a long holder, and kissed the women's hands, and they thought he was charming.

After dinner there would be another gathering. Some of the afternoon people might reappear, better dressed, but there would be people who had been specially invited: the author of a current best-seller, a well-known psychiatrist, an actress who was playing a leading role. The conversation would be lively, usually about politics, but it might be about psychoanalysis, or someone's trip abroad. Or even baseball . . . J. B. was an expert on the subject. If the discussion threatened to become too serious, if someone was disagreeing warmly, J. B. would throw in a remark that brought the talk around to the World Series. He had a favorite saying, "Stay loose," that came from baseball. He was a fan of the Reds . . . he grew up in Cincinnati.

Not everyone appreciated these diversions. "What is this American folly, bazeboll?" the Hungarian asked. He had been interrupted in the midst of a diatribe against the Soviet Union. People stared at him in silence. They were liberals . . . after this evening he was not invited back.

And Milly, J. B.'s wife, was not so mild. If there was a heated argument she would add fuel to the flames. She was like the Druid priestesses Tacitus describes, dressed in white robes, urging the warriors to battle. Then you saw that she had had one or two drinks too many. At this point J. B. would try to distract her, leading her aside. This would make her angry and her voice would rise. Mike Gallagher, my associate at the publishing house, told me that he had witnessed some late-night scenes that were sensational: a woman throwing the contents of her glass in another woman's face. Their husbands inviting each other to step outside.

❧

At our editorial conference J. B. clued us in on what people were reading these days and asked for book ideas. Scribner's were about to publish a novel about World War II, a blockbuster, the biggest thing since *The Naked and the Dead*. Rumor had it that the advance notices were excellent and that Scribner's were planning full-page ads. Where was our novel about World War II?

I recalled that some months ago, when two novels about the war were in the house and both Gallagher and I gave one of them very good reports, J. B. told us to forget it . . . no one was interested in the war these days.

J. B. was staring at me . . . was something wrong? No, I assured him, and he continued. There was a market for non-fiction adventure. Look at *Annapurna* and *Kon-Tiki*. Where, I said to myself, was our book about a raft?

That night at the Blue Mill, Gallagher's favorite restaurant, over steaks and french fries we discussed the conference. Had I noticed, Mike said, how many first novels by women we were publishing? J. B. met them at parties, women who'd published a story when they were in college and had written nothing since, not till J. B. discovered them.

"You do know, don't you, about J. B. and Frieda?"

I stared at him in astonishment.

"Didn't he ask you to let him use your apartment one afternoon?"

He had, as a matter of fact. To catch up on some reading. But I hadn't noticed anything, the apartment was just as I left it, nothing out of place.

What, Mike said, would I have expected to find if I'd known? Dirty bedsheets?

Hadn't I noticed that when he or I wrote a favorable book report, and Frieda disagreed, J. B. would invariably take her side? And that two of the books J. B. had signed contracts for recently we hadn't even seen, but Frieda liked them.

But the Burner, as Mike calls Frieda Bunsen, leaves to be an editor at another house, and we don't have to worry . . . the days flow smoothly again, reading manuscripts and writing reports.

Now and then I rise from my desk and go over to the window and look down a canyon to the Hudson and the funnels of ocean liners. I could take one and be back on the Left Bank, breathing the atmosphere of art . . . wine and Gaulois cigarette smoke. Or England . . . I saw very little of England during the war, only the green fields where we practiced platoon tactics and the dark, unlighted streets that led to the pub. But I don't have the price of the ticket . . . alimony and child support payments keep my nose glued to the job.

I am writing jacket copy for a historical novel set in Old Virginia. Barbara Cheveley is torn between her gratitude to Ronald Fairbough, a British captain of dragoons who saved her father's life, and her fascination with "Red Hugh" O'Malley, a smuggler with a price on his head. She does not know that O'Malley is, in fact, an officer in Washington's army, entrusted by the General with the most secret of missions, on which the fate of the army and the Revolution depends. The traitor Benedict Arnold plays a pivotal part in the story. In *Two Swords for Barbara Chevely* the author has given us once more the heady mixture of history and romance that won uncounted readers for *Traitor's Wife* and *Lord Lovat's Daughter*. Her new readers have a treat in store.

A shape looms over me . . . a stout woman with red hair, leaning on a cane. She lowers herself heavily on the chair next to my desk. She is holding a box in her lap . . . the manuscript, she says, I rejected . . . her biography of Elbert Hubbard. She stares at me, and I remember: when I opened the box there was a smell of mildew, and as I turned the pages a letter fell out, a letter of rejection dated . . . twenty years ago!

I try to think of something to say, and find myself using the words of our standard letter of rejection, about "the limitations of our budget." The red-haired woman continues to glower. Or is it a wig? She looks like Doctor Johnson. When I have finished speaking she leans forward. "Young man," she says, "you are a fool." For a moment the beautiful temptation flutters before me . . . it's not the first time I've seen her fanning her wings, the idea of simply saying to a writer, "Go to hell." But my paycheck puts a finger to her lips and I am silent. The biographer of Elbert Hubbard gathers her manuscript to her bosom, rises heavily, and lurches out. On the way she passes the office of Elizabeth O'Shaughnessy, our publicity woman, and leans in at the door . . . apparently she knows her. Betty looks up with a smile. "Don't smile at me with all your teeth, Miss O'Shaughnessy!" the old woman shouts, shaking her cane in the air, and makes an exit.

For some time Gallagher had been having an affair with the wife of a fashion photographer. She was given to taking off her clothes at parties. This didn't seem to bother her husband but it bothered Mike. He had always had a drinking problem but now he came late to work and would go out for a nip now and then. He dozed through the afternoon, slumped in his chair . . . you could actually hear him snore. Beatrice, the Office Manager's assistant, who sat at a desk across from me, slipped out to snitch on Mike.

J. B. had a heart-to-heart talk with Mike. He asked me to pitch in, to finish the anthology of love stories Mike had contracted to put together for the firm, and I wrote brief biographies of the authors. But the situation couldn't continue and J. B. had to let Mike go. He found a position as speech-writer for the president of CBS. Then he married an Italian who worked at the United Nations, and she took him with her to Rome.

Then J. B. left, to be an editor with a much bigger house. I visited him there and he showed me around. His office was palatial compared to the modest quarters he had previously occupied. There was a large bathroom adjoining his office, with a television set so that he could see the programs of the station that was affiliated with the publishing house. We were entering a new era, he told me; books would be aimed at television.

At a meeting of our staff with the new editor who was taking J. B.'s place I made an innocuous remark, and the Vice President in Charge of Sales turned on me savagely. "The trouble with you," he said, "is that you're sorry J. B. isn't here." I was taken aback. He continued in this vein . . . he must have been harboring venomous feelings towards me for some time. I had always detested him, with his foxy face and dapper suits, but I had thought he liked me. I used to listen to his stories about the publishing business.

I looked around the room. There wasn't one there who hadn't

been J. B.'s friend or pretended to be, and there wasn't one who had a good word to say about him now that he'd left. It was time for me to be leaving . . . not just this wretched bunch, I had to get out of the business. I had no interest in developing "book ideas," saw no reason to persuade someone to write a book if he didn't have the urge. And I felt the irony of helping others to write books when I should be writing my own. I wasn't cut out for a career in publishing.

I knew a man of my own age who was. At a party in the Village at which the usual faces were present, first-novelists and two or three who had a reputation, he explained that getting someone to write a book was simple: "You have to have a subject, then you write out what you know." It was evident, he said, when a writer didn't really know the subject. You could tell.

In that case, I thought, I'm not a writer, for I don't have a subject . . . mountain-climbing, crossing the Pacific on a raft, not even World War II. All I have is a love of writing, and it doesn't have to be my own.

There was one thing I could do. In order to supplement my income I had been teaching a section of English composition at Columbia, in the school of General Studies. I could go into teaching. I would have to obtain a Ph.D.—this was the prerequisite for teaching in a university, and any other kind would be drudgery. The G. I. Bill would pay for my courses and I could teach two sections of composition.

The woman with the red wig has had her revenge—I have not been able to put her out of my mind. Perhaps some people exist just to make an impression. She reappears, looming over me, shaking her walking stick. She is still carrying the box that contains the life of Elbert Hubbard. With her is the man who brought us a manuscript wrapped around with a chain and lock. When I asked him why, he said that for years Irving Berlin had been entering his apartment and stealing his songs.

There is the woman with the mating machine. In the picture it looks like an electric chair. You are to place your prospective mate in it and pull a switch. The pointer will swing so many degrees. You match this with your own score and make some calculations. Then you compare your friend's astrological sign with yours and consult a chart that tells you what to expect. Then you must consider: do you like each other? Are you compatible?

I told her that due to the limitations of our budget we could not publish her book. Her elbow began rapping on my desk and she trembled from head to toe. Beatrice slipped out of the door to warn the Office Manager that a crisis was impending. The woman with the mating machine spoke: "I hear you were in San Francisco."

Yes, I said, I had been there on my vacation.

"What," she said, "did they tell you about me?"

I see you too, old man with white hair and pince-nez glasses and little smile as though you have a secret. And indeed you do, an incredibly pornographic novel about young girls.

I see you all dimly, as manuscripts walking, spotted with mildew and soup stains. The despised and rejected. How much more interesting you were in person than the books you wrote!

Voices in the Plaza

Life is the best commentary, and no satire could be as cutting as a recent article about Jerry Rubin in the *New York Times*. It seems that Mr. Rubin, one of the leading activists of the Sixties, has discovered the joy of making money, and nowadays this is what he does. The rebel has become a yuppie, and anyone who didn't see it coming was a bit of a fool.

I certainly was. People of my generation that had lived through World War II, and settled down to a job and raising a family, thought the next generation would be braver than ours. "Don't trust anyone over thirty," Jack Weinberg said. To hear them, they would live on air and never do anything wrong.

I have never enjoyed politics—it's like going to the bathroom, something you have to do but not to be lingered over. In August 1964, however, I became involved. The President, Lyndon Johnson, seemed hell-bent on getting the United States into a shooting war. I was invited to sign an ad that appeared in the *San Francisco Chronicle*. It showed a Vietnamese man holding in his arms a child that had been burned by napalm, and it was headed, "The American people will bluntly and plainly call it murder . . . " The ad listed statements by congressmen who opposed the war, and called on the United Nations to reconvene the 1954 Geneva Conference in order to negotiate a settlement.

Some who had signed the ad were invited to appear on television and explain their reasons. One of the questions we were asked was: "Don't you think the President is better informed than you?" I said, "But he doesn't know how I feel." That evening I received a long-distance telephone call—Los Angeles? The John Birch society? The caller said, "We're going to get you." I told him I wasn't the pacifist he seemed to think I was—it was this war I objected to—and I owned a rifle. The next day I told a friend about the call and he said I should call the police. A Berkeley policeman, intelligent and conscientious, came to my house and took notes. I wouldn't be bothered anymore, he assured me—those people only tried to frighten you.

My dislike of the war made me sympathetic to the Free Speech Movement at Berkeley. This, the forerunner of student uprisings all over the country, began in the fall of '64. A Dean of Students announced that no tables, fund-raising, membership recruitment, or speeches would be permitted on the sidewalk at Bancroft and Telegraph. The heads of off-campus organizations formed a "united front" to protest the new ruling and requested the Dean's office to restore "free speech" and remove the various restrictions on free expression.

While we held our classes the voices of the student leaders could be heard in Sproul Plaza excoriating the Administration. Every few days brought a new crisis. On October 1 the police arrested Jack Weinberg and put him in a police car. The car was surrounded by a crowd so that it could not move; Mario Savio took off his shoes and climbed on top, and addressed the crowd while Weinberg sat inside looking out, being fed with milk and sandwiches as Elijah by the ravens.

On December 2, to the singing of Joan Baez seven hundred students marched into Sproul Hall and refused to leave. The next day the police carried them out, put them in wagons, and took them to jail. Bail was raised by voluntary contributions but the students would have to appear in court to answer charges. This was where I came in, with other members of the faculty: we formed a committee to provide legal assistance for the arrested students, that is, to hire lawyers and raise the money to pay their fees. While we discussed the wording of an appeal for contributions we could hear the voices of Mario Savio, Art Goldberg, Jackie Goldberg, and Bettina Aptheker, sounding in the Plaza. A professor on the other side of the table was speaking of revolutionary theory in Vienna forty years ago. He spoke tediously and long. "Bliss was it in that dawn to be alive / But to be young was very heaven." Hardly . . . but to be young certainly helped. The speakers in the Plaza were having all the fun.

One day I happened to be passing through New York, and a man I knew at the *Times* invited me to meet some important people, editors, managers, and trustees. They wanted to know what was happening at Berkeley. I told them . . . they listened politely, then talked of more important matters. People who lived in the Bay Area said it was the greatest place in the world, and we at the university thought our words had world-shaking consequences. But in the view of the *Times* they were not shaking so much as glasses on a sideboard.

But protests against the war did have an effect. They were like pebbles cast in a pool, sending out wider and wider ripples. A handful of people on a platform speaking against the war would show hundreds of others that it was possible to speak out—and some would resist the draft. At the same time, media coverage of the war brought it home to the people . . . the picture of a South Vietnamese officer shooting a prisoner in the head, the picture of a marine setting fire to a village with his cigarette lighter. Finally the average American got the point: Vietnam was the wrong place for Americans to be, and this was a war they could not win—unless they were willing to start World War III.

One day I spoke in the Plaza against the war. That evening there was to be a peace march to Oakland, with lighted candles, and I thought I could not urge others to act without acting myself,

so I went on the march. I found the way they marched annoying
. . . all out of step, in jerks and halts. The young woman beside
me lost a contact lens and I had to dissuade her from getting
down on hands and knees to look for it. As the candles moved into
Oakland people came out of their houses to see. "You people," a
resident said, shaking his head, "don't know what you have in this
country." Yes, I thought, but did not say—we had been warned
not to provoke anger—we know, and that's why we're marching,
in order to keep what we have.

Up ahead the Hell's Angels charged the line with their motor-
cycles. It was said that the Oakland police looked on while the
Angels were breaking arms and legs. Did this really happen? I
don't know . . . maybe it did. The Oakland police were not like
the police in Berkeley—they were your average hippie-hating cops.

At a poetry reading against the war at Longshoreman's Hall in
San Francisco we anticipated some further violence by the Hell's
Angels, but Allen Ginsberg went and talked to them, and came
back to report that they were a bunch of "sweet guys." And in fact
they didn't appear again to molest peace-marchers. There was
some talk, reported in a San Francisco underground newspaper,
The Oracle, of mollifying the police too by raising their consciousness. They might be "equipped with the words and mystique of
an ancient mantra still used in India to disperse crowds and multitudes." The hippies were already wearing buttons that said,
"LOVE A COP" and "TEACH A COP TO FUCK."

But nothing came of these attempts to love their enemies and
teach their enemies to love them—the police continued to disperse crowds and multitudes by using clubs, hoses, and paddy
wagons.

I took part in several poetry readings against the war. These
left me with mixed feelings, for I loved my country and found it
hard to listen to those who obviously didn't. I remember one poet
at a rally in Philadelphia who, upon mounting the platform,
pointed to the flag and said, "Get that rag out of here!" What, I
thought, am I doing in the company of such *canaille*?

During these years my tax returns were audited and I was gouged a few thousand extra tax dollars, on one pretext or another. This was Richard Nixon's way of punishing those who protested against his administration. A man came to my house seeking information about a student who had applied for a government job. As his eyes darted here and there I realized it wasn't the student information was wanted about, but me.

I see Richard Nixon these days sitting in the stands at ball games—the TV camera picks out the spoon-nosed, lantern-jawed profile. What is he doing there? Why isn't he in jail?

Yesterday, Allen Ginsberg said, he had seen Mario Savio weeping. Saying he wanted to go out and live in nature.

Beautiful, said Timothy Leary.

So I mean, Ginsberg said, he's basically where we are: stoned.

Activist and flower children had a lot in common. But the activists wanted to change the System, flower children just wanted to be left alone.

IN THE WIND: a 130-acre ranch for use as combination farm, ashram, center for Human Be-Ins, country fairs, dances . . . a cooperative marketplace in the Haight-Ashbury, to distribute farm products, crafts, health foods, etc. . . . .

Gary Snyder told how he'd dropped out and survived, and this was before there was a "community." It meant "mastering all kinds of techniques of living really cheap." He would get free rice off the docks, spilled from sacks when they were being forklifted. He had it worked out with the guards to gather fifteen or twenty-five pounds of rice for him, and also tea. He'd pick this up and take it around and give it to friends.

"We used to go around at one or two in the morning, around the Safeways and Piggly Wigglies in Berkely, with a shopping bag, and hit the garbage cans out in back. We'd get Chinese cabbage, lots of broccoli and artichokes that were thrown out because they didn't look sellable anymore. So I never bought any vegetables for the three years I was a graduate student at Berkeley. When I ate meat, it was usually horse meat from the pet store."

Activists and flower children came together for a Human Be-In on the Polo Grounds of Golden Gate Park. Let *The Oracle* tell it:

> And with the sun setting, Allen Ginsberg and Gary Snyder chant the night with the Om Sri Maitreya mantrum, turned toward the sun, double disks revolving in the red-gold glare, small groupings arms linked moving gently from side to side. She a beautiful Nubian princess, he a motorcycle wizard and warlock, and I poet and participant, swaying, good people, Om Sri Maitreya. The sun moving down behind the trees, heading for the Pacific . . .

Shall we leave it there with activists and flower children gently moving from side to side, Om Sri Maitreya Om?

Yes, it would be best to leave, before Ginsberg puts on a suit and tie, and Leary is an old man telling stories to lunch clubs, and Jerry Rubin discovers how nice it is to have money.

Baruch

You entered the incorporated village of Belle Terre through white gateposts with an American eagle atop each post. A "French Provincial" gate house had been designed by the architect Stanford White who was shot dead one night at Madison Square Garden in the middle of the show.

White had a protégé, the artists' and photographers' model, Evelyn Nesbit. But White was a married man, so she married Harry Thaw. She gave Thaw an account of her seduction by White, with champagne and a red velvet swing, that filled him with an irresistible impulse to shoot Stanford White. This was the defense offered by Thaw's attorneys, and it worked: he was committed to an asylum for the insane.

Our house was to the left of the gate. Built in 1916, it stood four-square, so square that it looked functionally modern. It was solidly built, the living room and dining room paneled in chestnut, a tree now obsolete. There were three stories with plenty of space, and a garage separate from the house with a room above it that I used as my study.

Belle Terre was quiet. The houses half-hidden among leaves gave no sign of life. You could walk in the lanes for an hour without hearing a voice . . . only the chirping of birds, rustling of squirrels, the fall of a dead branch. Across the Sound the shoreline of

Connecticut was visible. A ferry plied between Bridgeport and Port Jefferson just down the road. We were far from New York City . . . there were sixty miles between. Sea and sky hadn't changed since the poet described them a hundred years ago:

> hurrying tumbling waves, quick-broken crests,
> slapping,
> The strata of color'd cloud, the long bar of maroon-
> tint away solitary by itself, the spread of purity
> it lies motionless in,
> The horizon's edge, the flying sea-crow, the fragrance
> of salt marsh and mud.

An incorporated village . . . after a while I understood what these words meant: *Keep Out!* The real estate developers who planned Belle Terre at the beginning of the century envisioned a community of millionaires, excluding "inharmonious elements." The Village Board were keeping up the tradition: they had recently voted not to have sidewalks even though this presented a danger to pedestrians, especially children, from passing cars. But if there were sidewalks strangers would be tempted to come into the village and go walking about. *They* might start coming in.

I was walking Tippy and Lady one afternoon when a car drew up and stopped. A young man was driving with a woman of sixty in a fur coat. He asked if there were a house for sale in the area. I said that I thought there was. He said, "You have a very attractive place here." I agreed that it was. He said, "I see they haven't moved in yet." I considered this. "No," I said, "but we're working on it, trying to make this a part of America." The woman seemed startled . . . "We're Americans too," she said. The young man stared straight ahead and drove off.

I went over to the university two or three times a week to meet my classes and hold conference hours. Sometimes there was also a committee meeting I ought to go to, but not often, for there were faculty members who liked to be on committees and run the department. *Apparatchiki.* The rest of us could go home.

I was never the kind of teacher who liked to sit in his office and talk to students about their problems . . . my thoughts were about the subject I was teaching. If I could say something true about an author's work I felt I had done my job. I didn't stay at the university any longer than I had to. Besides, the place was depressing: though it was in the process of construction it looked like some ancient ruined city.

Construction had begun in the early sixties. Stony Brook was to be a great research center. Buildings went up in a hurry and they were already deteriorating. When it rained the books in the library had to be covered with sheets of polyethylene.

The buildings were a jumble of different styles. Some were made of brick in the vaguely "Georgian" style used on Long Island for high schools and other public buildings. Others were of concrete with windows that didn't open . . . the atmosphere of a tomb. If the body shows the soul, what kind of soul must the people who built the university have?

The students were demoralized. Many were in the university only to avoid being drafted and sent to Vietnam. They lived in dirty, crowded dormitories and there was no off-campus area where they were welcome . . . a street where they might drink a few beers, have a cheap meal, go to a movie. No Telegraph Avenue. The police raided a dormitory and netted some students who smoked marijuana. This made newspaper headlines.

The new university had a reputation for radical experiment. One teacher gave all his students A's. Another passed out pornographic pictures to the class. Such teachers were as demoralized as their students.

These were the years when American bombers were killing people in villages halfway around the world. It was hard to uphold authority when the highest authority in the land was waging a war that had not been voted by Congress—when the generals lied to the President, and the President lied to the people.

❧

They married and lived in houses; they had children, drove cars, went to work, shopped in supermarkets, and watched TV. Poetry hardly ever spoke of this . . . it did not speak of such lives except with irony and contempt. But I was one of those people . . . the only thing that made me different was being a writer. I wanted to speak of the life I had and tell stories about the men and women I knew. The stories would be in verse, for this was what I enjoyed . . . the rhythm of the line.

But if I did write such poems who would read them? At the end of the nineteenth century Mallarmé said that poems were made with words, not ideas, and this was the kind of poetry we had been getting ever since. I am exaggerating, there were exceptions, but the poetry that was called "modern" and discussed by critics and scholars was the kind Mallarmé recommended. It was the lyric and it had very little to say about ordinary existence. It did not narrate . . . it was hermetic. Ideas were conveyed so indirectly that a critic was needed to explain them. This made work for critics but the greater part of life went unexpressed.

I was setting out on a lonely road. The people my poems were about, my next door neighbors, wouldn't read them . . . they preferred television. Editors blamed poets for being obscure and not writing for the common reader, but when I sent one of those editors a poem with character and incident, written in language any reader could understand, it was promptly rejected . . . it wasn't "poetic" enough. Over the years *The New Yorker* had published a number of my poems . . . I had contracted to let them see my work before I showed it to anyone else. The poems I sent them now were returned and I tore up the contract.

There was no precedent for the kind of poetry I wanted to write. Some years ago I had broken with rhyme and meter and learned to write in free form. Now I discarded the traditional ornaments of language, especially metaphors. I wanted to render the thing itself exactly as it happened.

I discovered what writers of novels and short stories knew: if you had a point of view everything seemed to fall into place and move. Therefore the hard work had to be done on myself, understanding what I felt and what I wanted to say. Then I could tell a story and it could be believed.

I received some help, but not from a poet. When I was a child my mother used to tell stories about the village in Russia where she was born. She talked about people in the family . . . the man who was some sort of revolutionist and who hid under the mattress on which his wife was lying; the police looked everywhere but under the mattress, and so he escaped. His wife was going to have a baby, and the police wouldn't go near her . . . they thought it would bring bad luck.

When I went to college I read Russian novels. Gogol's *Dead Souls* made me think that in some ways Russia and America were alike: they both had large spaces and unpredictable characters, and there was a movement of the whole, to an end that was not in sight.

> And you, Russia of mine—are you not also speeding, like a *troika* which nothing can overtake? . . . Where, then, are you speeding . . . ? Where? Answer me! But no answer comes—only the weird sound of your collar-bells.

An American novelist had written of whaling in similar terms: "whatever swift, rushing thing I stood on was not so much bound to any haven ahead as rushing from all havens astern." I was a voyager myself; I had left the island where I was born and was moving into the unknown. These American and Russian writers appealed to me in a way that the literature of England, with its emphasis on social relations, did not. Americans and Russians were more romantic.

Now I was reading Chekhov. He knew how to tell a story about ordinary people who turned out to be extraordinary. I invented characters and placed them in Russian settings. I wrote about Isidor who hid under a mattress, and Dvonya:

> I love her black hair, and eyes
> as green as a salad
> that you gather in August . . .

Avram the cello-mender:

> the only Jewish sergeant
> in the army of the Tsar.

and Meyer the student:

> Dark roofs of Volhynia,
> do you remember Meyer
> who went to the University?

Then I applied what I had learned from Chekhov to writing poems with American settings, and of course it worked just as well as in the "Russian" poems.

One poem, "Baruch," gave me particular satisfaction, for it brought Russia and America together. It was the story of a man in Russia who owned a hat factory. The character was based on my mother's father who owned a brick factory and one of her sisters who had a knack for making hats. I called the character Baruch and gave him a desire: he wanted to study the Torah. One night the factory burned down, leaving him free to study. But as the old saying has it, "Prophecy is too great a thing for Baruch," and he fell sick and died. The poem then moved to a young woman named Deborah who was addicted to reading great authors.

> The question was, which would she marry,
> Tolstoy or Lermontov or Pushkin?

A rich man with a team of horses came from Kiev to court her, and her family persuaded her to marry him, but on the wedding night she sent him packing.

The third part took place in America, and now it was clearly my own story.

> We have been devoted to words.
> Even here in this rich country
> Scripture enters and sits down
> and lives with us like a relative.
> Taking the best chair in the house . . .

His eyes go everywhere, not missing anything.
Wherever his looks go, something ages
and suddenly tears or falls.
Here, a worn place in the carpet,
there a crack in the wall.

I was writing about the part that learning played in my life. No
matter how carefully you have built for yourself and your wife and
children there seems to be something incompatible between the
life of the family and the life in books. When the word enters and
sits down the house trembles. "For behold, the Lord comman-
deth, and he will smite the great house with breaches and the little house with clefts."

3

A Window

> . . . life is much more successfully looked at from a
> single window, after all.
>
> *The Great Gatsby*

Breezy and cold, a sun like a diamond blazing so that you
can't look at it . . . the trees and hedge in front of my window are
dark shapes. When I think that every day of my life I look at the
sky and earth directly, it's a blessing.

It says to me, Write! But it doesn't say what about. That is
where nature leaves off, cuts the towline . . . where work starts and
those who can't do it fall astern. Up ahead are the great ships
going into the blue.

Miriam comes back from the walk she takes every afternoon
and stops by my study to press her face to the glass and make a
mouth like a goldfish. These are the whims that make life worth
living. There are people who know this, and then there are the
others who provide us with our daily quota of bad news.

Aristotle said that humanity is the animal that lives in a *polis*.
How about, the animal that makes faces?

Love in the West

The sun is shining, the sky is blue, there are people on the beach. Libero, who is in charge of the bagno "Antaura," makes us welcome, and Maximo the beach boy sets up an umbrella and brushes the sand off two deck chairs. Miriam stretches out on a towel and I sit writing these notes.

There's a sea of umbrellas colored orange, yellow, green, and blue. The Apuan Alps . . . pale blue, jagged peaks rising against clouds racked and piled in a sky bluer than the mountains. The clouds are shaded violet and gray, but there to the right, over the long back of a mountain, stands a puff of white cloud.

The Moroccans are going by. This one has dresses to sell; another, a case of sunglasses and combs; a third, sunglasses and watches.

And there are people . . . faces and bodies. Denis de Rougemont, whose *Love in the Western World* I have been reading, says that we are sold the idea of a standardized beauty, which changes with the generations. Our search for the person who will satisfy our craving for the ideal makes us reject any love that is possible. This is the myth of Tristan and Isolde. " . . . to love love more than the object of love, to love passion for its own sake, has been to love to suffer . . . Passionate love, the longing for what sears and annihilates us in its triumph—there is the secret which Europe has never

88

The Simpson family in Jamaica, c. 1891. *Left to right:* Aston, the author's father; Inis, Aston's sister; Aston's parents, James Montague Simpson and Emily Laselve; his sisters May and Edith. Aston's brother Bertie is not in the picture.

The Marantz family in Lutsk, Russia, c. 1905. *To the left:* Rosalind, the author's mother. Her mother, Pearl, in the center with her second husband, Lazar.

Aston Simpson in the Jamaican Reserve Regiment, c. 1914. The Webley service revolver was not worn on this occasion.

The author's mother as
an aspiring opera singer.
New York City, c. 1914.

The author with his
older brother, Herbert.
Jamaica c. 1927.

Rosalind in the thirties.

The Meccano Club with the chapel in the background, Munro College, Jamaica. The author is in the second row, fourth from the left.

In the 101st Airborne Division. London, July 1944.

Poets in the sixties: James Wright, Louis Simpson, Robert Bly.

Louis and Miriam at their wedding, June 1985.

Miriam with Willa, Louis with Custis Lee. Setauket, 1989.

My father's house. Jamaica, 1992.

allowed to be given away; a secret it has always repressed—and preserved! Hardly anything could be more tragic . . . "

Marriage would mean the end of passion, and so adultery is glorified. This leads to suffering and death. Rougemont offers a solution: one should marry and stay married with a passion that would be equal and superior to adultery. The trouble with most marriages is that people enter into them lightly. He appears to be saying that you should only fall in love with the person you can stay in love with.

Easier said than done! People will fall in love with people they shouldn't. The Greeks knew this . . . so did the authors of *Phèdre* and *Remembrance of Things Past*. So, for that matter, does every middle-aged man and woman on the beach.

It's more a matter of luck than he thinks. Speaking of love . . . I received a letter from a friend saying that I'd left my best poem out of my *Collected Poems*, the one titled "Cliff Road."

It is about Belle Terre where I lived for ten years, and also, it seems, about my state of mind.

> Walking on the road at night . . .
> At regular intervals a street light
> makes a green shelf in the leaves.
> Houses give off a muffled sound—
> TV, the murmur of voices
> and roar of the studio audience.
>
> From time to time a plane goes winking over,
> heading for Kennedy or La Guardia.
>
> You pass the house of Angelo Scalise
> who came here from Chicago—
> the biggest house on the street.
> It seems there is always a limousine
> parked near the gate, with a driver
> who, when you pass, glances up.

Then the cottage back in the trees
inhabited by the Henderson sisters . . .
I have often seen them together
in the winter gathering sticks.

Then there is a slope and a path
that goes right down to the beach.
The fishers are sure to be there
surfcasting, in absolute silence,
side by side but at a distance.

They start casting at Connecticut
in the sunset at high tide
when the shore seems to be drifting.
Then it's dark, you no longer see them
but, as I said, they are there
you can tell, by a faint white splash.

The road itself continues,
narrowing. This is Lovers' Lane.
It ends at a fence on a cliff,
looking at the lights on the opposite shore.

"Cliff Road" speaks of a time in my life that I don't want to
remember . . . of wanhope and despair. The description of Belle
Terre at night, the closed, hushed atmosphere, is also a description of the life of the observer. But I should have ended with the
fishermen and the splash of the line in the dark. The lines that follow are an intrusion of the poet's rather limited view. Cliff Road
narrows to Lovers' Lane, and this "ends at a fence on a cliff, / looking at the lights on the opposite shore." The poem suggests that
love is a dead end and yearning for a happiness that is always
beyond our reach. It's "on the opposite shore."

This is the conclusion and it just isn't true. Or it is true only for
the speaker in the poem. This, of course, raises the question of

truth and poetry. We have often been told that poets are liars, meaning that they make up things and these are not to be judged by ordinary standards. Yes, and when poetry is written as fiction it would be absurd to complain that it takes liberties with the facts. Imagination has its own truths that can be far more illuminating than observations of "life."

It would be different if "Cliff Road" were a story . . . the idea being expressed would be part of the story. But the idea comes at you straight . . . the feeling that love is hopeless seems to be the poet's and to be taken at face value. But, as I've said, it isn't true: love doesn't have to be a dead end. On the contrary, for many people it's an opening into the universe.

The poem, as Gatsby would say, is just personal, and I think I was right to exclude it.

Struga Evenings

On the first evening the poets read from a bridge above a river. The people were in their best clothes. They had come to hear the foreign poets.

A poet from Georgia in the Soviet Union delivered his poem in a stentorian voice, with operatic gestures.

Each of us read one poem. There was no translation and the audience could have understood very little, but they applauded anyway.

In the morning we were transported by bus from the hotel to the auditorium. There was a display of books in the foyer. Books by poets from the U.S.S.R., Poland, Hungary, Rumania, East Germany, Czechoslovakia, Holland, Italy, Denmark, Sweden, and England were on display. But no books by the poets from the United States.

The wife of the American ambassador was introduced to the American poets. She explained that the ambassador hadn't been able to come . . . he had another engagement. She had never heard of any of us and seemed surprised that there were American poets. She looked rather bewildered by the crowd, the reporters and television cameras. For something called a poetry festival!

There were headphones at every seat and simultaneous translation. The subject to be discussed was poetry and politics. Poets from Poland, Rumania, Czechoslovakia and so on went up to the platform and read into the microphones a speech that had been carefully prepared saying that it was the duty of the writer to serve society.

I had lunch with a woman poet from East Germany. A man in a double-breasted suit came with us and listened to everything we were saying. The East Germans had received two invitations to the festival, so they gave one place to a poet, the other to a policeman.

When we returned to the auditorium one of the people in charge told the American poets that people were saying they hadn't taken part in the proceedings. So I went up to the platform and made a speech. I said that American poets had opposed the war in Vietnam, and not because it was their duty but because they felt they had to. If you had faith in the people why couldn't you let them make up their own minds?

When I left the platform a man asked me if I were willing to be interviewed. I said yes, and he took me to a room where television was set up. The interviewer wanted to talk about the opposition to the war in Vietnam. When the interview was over he gave me a form to sign. Then he took out his wallet, counted off banknotes, and put them in my hand. Direct action . . . It was not what I had expected to find under Socialism.

That evening the hotel put on a special treat for dinner, the red trout for which Lake Ohrid is famous. On the way to the dining room I encountered some writers from Rumania, Hungary, and so on. They gave me a big smile and one shook my hand. Later I was told that the leader of the Soviet delegation had said that I made a good speech. So it was OK to smile.

✦

My speech was reported in the morning newspaper . . . the part about American poets being opposed to the war. But they left out the part about letting people think for themselves.

The subject this morning was translation. In the afternoon I went down to the lake with Merwin and Carolyn Kizer. The poet from Georgia, the one who bawled his poem from the bridge on the first evening, came down to the beach with his wife. They were stout and white. They stood in the lake and soaped themselves. That's what they thought it was for . . . to take a bath in.

The poets were reading in the evening. I missed the bus but a man offered me a lift in his car. He was with his wife. Their name, he said, was Drakul. It was a historic name . . . the original owners of the name had lived in a castle a few hundred miles to the north. He was a translator by profession.

On the way we had a flat and had to change the tire. I looked around for a stone to stop the car from rolling but there was none in sight. Down the road there was a wall with a gate. I walked though the gate and found myself in a farmyard. There was a stone in the middle of the yard. An old woman dressed in black was sitting at the door of the farmhouse. I told her that I was just going to borrow the stone and would bring it back. I spoke French, thinking she might understand it better than English. She said nothing but watched as I picked it up and carried it away. Her stone.

✦

After the morning discussion in the auditorium, what about I don't remember, I went into town to the travel office. They told me that my return flight was confirmed.

In the open-air market they were selling pottery, jewelry, lace, and embroidery. I asked the price of a piece of lace. The man named a price and I gave him the money and took the lace. He followed me, talking Macedonian. He seemed to be trying to tell me something.

I thought about it later. He must have named a price far above what he expected to get. He expected me to bargain with him as usual and bring down the price. When I gave him what he'd asked for he was astonished. I had upset his system of doing business.

He had followed me trying to explain that he was an honest man, not a thief.

Three women in trousers came striding from higher ground down to the market. The trousers were bagged and tied at the ankle. They were brown-skinned . . . Turks or Gypsies, but not like the little Gypsy women you see in Italy who come quickly with their children down a street, begging and stealing everything that isn't nailed down. These were big women . . . they walked with strides and looked capable of lifting a man off his feet with one arm or knocking him senseless with a blow of the fist.

When I returned to the hotel a female professor and her husband who lived in Struga asked me to have dinner at their house. They had also invited Serge Fauchereau, a French writer with a special interest in contemporary American poetry. And there was an editor from a Yugoslav publishing house.

They served dinner early so there would be time to go to the poetry-reading. It was a good dinner though there seem to be no green vegetables in Macedonia, only tomatoes, cucumbers, and rice. There is always plenty of wine.

The man from the publishing house asked if Serge and I would do an anthology of contemporary American verse. It would be translated and published throughout Yugoslavia. We said that we would and everyone was happy, toasting the project in slivovitz.

This was the last morning of the festival at Struga and no discussion was scheduled, so that the visitors could go sightseeing.

Some of the poets would be going on to other places on a poetry-reading tour, finishing at Skopje. One of the people in charge asked me to join the group. I said that I was sorry but I had to leave tomorrow. I had told them so when I accepted their invitation, and they had agreed. I was sorry but I had to be getting back to London . . . my family was expecting me.

He said that he was sorry I couldn't be with the group, but he understood.

I went to the travel office in Struga to pick up my ticket. There was no record of a reservation, and no seat immediately available. There might be one in two or three days.

There was nothing for it but to go with the group.

On the last evening they were giving a medal to W. H. Auden and he would be reading his poems. So I didn't go. I disliked the poet who said that poetry was "fundamentally frivolous" (one of his admirers, John Hollander, once told me that all good poetry was camp). At eleven people came straggling back to the hotel, looking subdued. They had been treated to the later Auden.

I sat on the veranda overlooking the lake. Bogamil Jusil who had organized the festival was there. So were Serge and Carolyn, and the Swedish poet Lars Gustaffson. Merwin may have been there too . . . I don't remember. We sat up all night talking and drinking. Now and then someone would join the group and someone would leave. We stayed until dawn broke and the English couple came by on their way to the lake.

The group traveled in three limousines. They drove fast and almost as fast on the turns. We were going up a mountain. The partisans had fought the Germans from the mountains where planes and tanks couldn't get at them.

We gave a reading of our poems in a room with rows of chairs. Then we had lunch at an inn, sitting outdoors. There was a painting of a window on one side of the wall of the inn, to match the real window on the other side. I ate a cucumber and tomato salad . . . I'd have liked some spinach.

While we were having lunch a wedding party came walking on the dirt road that wound around the mountain, a fiddler playing in front. The bride was in a white dress, the groom in a blue serge suit. They arrived at the inn and everyone had to toast the bride and groom. It might have been like this in Russia where my mother came from. Perhaps they would paint a window on a wall.

We drove across a plain where there were long-horned cattle. It looked like Texas. I was surprised at the size of the country.

There were wrecked vehicles, cars and trucks, even a bus, along the highway going to Skopje.

Our last reading was at the university in Skopje. After the reading the man in charge of the tour came to me and said that the misunderstanding about my ticket had been cleared up. He was able . . . he was happy to be able to say that a place had been found for me on the flight leaving in the morning.

That was how the system worked. They didn't say that you had to stay with the group . . . they just made it impossible to do anything else.

Serge and I put together the anthology of contemporary American verse, with an introduction, and it was translated and published in Yugoslavia. Years later when I visited Serge at his house in Coye-la-forêt he showed me a copy . . . his only copy, in case I had ideas. Neither of us ever heard from the publisher. There was nothing we could do about it, short of going to Yugoslavia.

Maybe we shall some day and spend the royalties on slivovitz, if the publisher hasn't spent them himself.

The House of the Stare

Come build in the empty house of the stare.

W. B. Yeats

I'm back to looking out the window. To my left there's a
woodpile, a fence, and a view of our neighbor's roof. Directly in
front, a patch of grass with an azalea, a dogwood, and some ever-
greens that screen our garbage cans from the street. There are
two beds of vegetables with wire around them to keep Willa and
Custis out. Moving to the right . . . the square end of the hedge,
the driveway, and a perspective of grass running up to the street.
In the distance, tall trees against the sky. The view is framed on
the right by a birch tree and a corner of the house.

The view changes from day to day and season to season. Today,
the tenth of May, the azalea is robed like a prince of the Church
in deep, almost purple red. The slender dogwood lifts arms with
pink blossoms as though offering an oblation. It sways in the
wind. I wouldn't be too surprised if it floated away from the earth
and danced.

For years after I left California I couldn't put my finger on just
what it was I hadn't liked about the place. I thought, the absence
of history . . . at least, any that mattered to me. But that wasn't
the whole answer. A few weeks ago Miriam and I were in
California, driving to San Francisco from Sonoma and Napa
where we'd been looking at vineyards. As we approached the city

I knew what it was . . . the barren hills. Rows of ticky-tacky houses perched on what seem to be mounds of mud. A green more like mold than grass and no trees. In Berkeley when I lived there we had tall redwoods right in our yard, but in general the landscape of California is bare, and "I love no leafless land."

I go to the bookshelves to see if I have the line right, and find myself caught up in the book. When I was an adolescent I was much taken with Housman's poems. His pessimistic views, expressed with such music, appealed to me. I had the liking for tragedy that you have at fifteen when you know that all the bad things will happen to other people. You are trying on different roles, and self-pity is most pleasing. Reading Housman I could see myself as a forsaken lover or a soldier going overseas to be slain in battle.

I owned his books in pocket editions I'd sent away for to England. I would take one out to the willows and read.

> On russet floors, by waters idle,
> The pine lets fall its cone;
> The cuckoo shouts all day at nothing
> In leafy dells alone;
> And traveller's joy beguiles in autumn
> Hearts that have lost their own.

Within a year of reading Housman I had become modern: I was reading T. S. Eliot and D. H. Lawrence. Today the author of *The Plumed Serpent* reminds me of a tour guide. He is wearing a pith helmet and khaki shorts that expose knobby knees and scrawny legs. His white skin is blistered and peeling. He is delivering a lecture on Quetzalcoatl to a group of schoolteachers from Muncie, Indiana, and telling them how rotten they are because they think with their heads and not with their solar plexuses. The women think he's the cat's pajamas. The men hope they'll be going back soon to the hotel and be able to slip away for a drink.

Eliot, however, has held up. I don't think much of him personally—he was a snob and racist—but when he wrote "Prufrock" and "The Waste Land" he surpassed himself. If five hundred years from now people are still reading English they'll be reading these poems. There is music here too, of another kind, and the images are fascinating. "The Waste Land" is about images.

> . . . you know only
> A heap of broken images, where the sun beats,
> And the dead tree gives no shelter, the cricket no relief,
> And the dry stone no sound of water.

We have lived among images, we are bombarded with images and confused by our senses. The thunder tells us plainly, "Give. Sympathize. Control." We know the way out of the waste land but lack the will to take it.

Going to bookshelves to check a quotation can be distracting. As I sit looking out the window I'm conscious of all the authors on the shelves behind me. Sometimes I feel they're encouraging . . . at other times I hear them saying, "What's the use? No one reads us. What make you think they'll want to read you?" There stand Chaucer, Chekhov, Jane Austen, hundreds of poets, and the author of "Enoch Soames." How many students, how many professors of English, have even heard of "Enoch Soames"? And if the professors don't read literature, and most of them don't— they're too busy reading literary theory to read literature—what about the people who aren't in a university?

Is the House of Fiction closing down? The door only opens inward, and what if the key never turns? What will become of the characters? Will they stay forever in the dark?

> father, mother, child
> With painted eyes,
> How sad it is to be a little puppet!

On what page will they be? In which chapter? It's like the argument over the Last Judgment: when the world comes to an end and you are given the body you will have for all eternity, which you will you be? The one you were at twenty? At sixty? Or at five?

Suppose you were left eternally in a room by Robbe-Grillet with no one to talk to, only the furniture. Or in a storm at sea, forever pitching and rolling. Or at Gettysburg on the third day, among the troops waiting on Seminary Ridge. What if you are running all over Yonville trying to borrow money. Or, a few pages later, writhing in the throes of arsenic poisoning. And no one ever turns the page.

But I'm looking at it from the reader's point of view. We think we give the characters life. We're accustomed to picking them up and putting them down . . . sometimes in the middle of a sentence. And we think they ought to be grateful. But suppose they are the ones with life and we the illusion? Fernando Pessoa remarks, "There are images in the secret corners of books that live more clearly than many men and women. There are literary phrases that possess an absolutely human individuality."

I don't want to drive it into the ground, but fiction is more interesting, more alive, than most people's lives. Would you rather talk to Jane Austen's Emma or to Kimberly B. Watlington who, the *New York Times* informs me, is engaged to David Michael Bernard. "Miss Watlington, a marketing consultant at James Madison financial Services in Philadelphia, graduated from Philips Exeter Academy and Smith College. She received an M. B. A. from Dartmouth College. Her father, who is retired, was a business manager at the Springfield, Mass., office of Alamen, a diversified electronics and industrial manufacturing company." These aren't people and marriages, they are assets and mergers.

So life will continue in the House of Fiction. And as reality is with the characters I don't think they'll mind if people stop reading. They're probably looking forward to the day when the "reading public" will disappear. It can't come a day too soon. They'll no longer be tied like serfs to the page. They'll be free to move . . . to a different chapter or right out of the book.

Many would prefer to be by a different author. The character in a novel by Dostoievsky will be able to move to *Dead Souls* and have a good laugh for a change. How good, after those endless discussions of the soul, to observe Chichikov cutting a figure in provincial society!

Easily and gracefully did he exchange agreeable badinage with one lady, and then approach another one with the short, mincing steps usually affected by young-old dandies who are fluttering around the fair. As he turned, not without dexterity, to right and left, he kept one leg slightly dragging behind the other, like a short tail or a comma. This trick the ladies particularly admired.

Miss Havisham has been sitting *shiva* in her wedding dress, clamped to a chair. Now she's free to run and shout. What a pleasure to go to the toilet . . . to have a bath! She would like her hair restyled . . . to wear a Christian Lacroix creation.

And the brave artillery captain . . .

> The brave artillery captain
> who stands there taking the blame
> for the Battle of Schöngraben
> is thinking, "You can take your cannon
> and stick them all up your ass.
>
> Why should I 'stay in character'
> and 'contribute to the plot'?
> Anton Pavlovich [that's Chekhov]
> told me, the last time he came,
> he had an opening, just made
>
> for a steady fellow like me:
> as a merchant with a fat wife,
> two daughters who like fine clothes,
> a son who's a gambler and drunkard,
> a mistress who wants a dacha . . .
>
> On second thought, I suppose
> 'Better the devil you know,'
> as they say, 'than the one you don't.'
> I'll just stay with the battery
> and try to do better next time."

✤

It's been raining all afternoon in gusts, like hurricane weather though this isn't the season. It isn't unpleasant . . . on the contrary, rather exciting. I left the study and went into the house at five. As I came in there was a rumbling of thunder and Custis went by, tail down, heading for the basement. At the faintest sound of thunder he's off. If it thunders during the night I'll be waked by the shaking of the lamp next to the bed. It's Custis shaking, wedged in the corner between the lamp and the wall. Willa isn't so affected, only if it's a full-fledged thunderstorm with flashes of lightning and cracks of thunder. Then she'll make her way up to the bedroom too. Veronica, on the other hand, didn't mind thunder a bit. Miriam thinks this is because she was raised as a pup not to mind it. The children used to sit up with her and say, "Look at the lightning!"

Or maybe it was in Veronica's nature not to mind. She was a Westie and small but she had a great heart. She took a dislike to the United Parcel Service and would bark furiously when the uniform appeared to make a delivery. She ran from one window to another barking. The driver was in terror of her . . . he'd throw the package onto the porch and hurry back to his van. Miriam asked him why, since there was glass between him and the dog. He said, "You never know."

One afternoon on our walk with the dogs we passed through the wood where houses were being built. A German Shepherd appeared with a paper bag in his mouth, the leftovers of some workman's lunch. The dog seemed mightily pleased with himself. Ron didn't hesitate . . . she charged. The Shepherd must have been five times her size, but he took one glance at the bundle of white fury coming at him, dropped his bag lunch, and fled into the wood.

Every morning Ron would wait outside while I finished breakfast. When I appeared she would turn around and lead the way to the study, and she stayed with me all morning while I worked. She didn't take easily to people but she took to me, I think because

I didn't try to make her like me. She gave Willa a wide berth . . .
Willa growled at her. But Ron and Custis were companions, looking to each other for approval when they ran to the door and
barked. Before Veronica came to live here Custis wouldn't come
into the study; he didn't like being cooped up. But now that
Veronica is no longer here he has taken her place and sits in a
chair while I work.

She is buried on the slope where she liked to sit and watch
whatever was passing.

Tonight Inspector Morse was on TV . . . not a good episode, a far-
fetched and complicated plot about a Japanese visitor to Oxford
and some people intent on revenging an atrocity committed by
the Japanese during World War II. The interest of the series is in
the character of the Inspector and the by-play between him and
Sergeant Lewis, but the British scriptwriter made the mistake,
common with American scriptwriters, of relying on a plot and
heaping violence on violence in order to hold the interest of the
audience. It left you with the feeling of having been confused with
details and cheated of a story.

The scriptwriter managed to get in two dirty cracks about
America. One was about the American government's protecting
a war criminal because he was an expert on the effects of poison
gas. The other was about the Atom Bomb being dropped on
Hiroshima and Nagasaki . . . some day the Japanese might exact
a dire revenge.

British television is loaded with remarks of this kind, for it
employs a number of people who dislike the United States for one
reason or another. One reason is that in the States intellectuals,
that is, writers, aren't held in great respect. An Englishman with a
good education may not be of the upper class but he can feel
superior to many people who don't have his command of language. To such a person democracy is repugnant . . . in the States
he'd have less respect than a plumber or electrician.

Another reason is that many British intellectuals are politically to the Left. At this point they must be rather discomfited: Marxism hasn't turned out to be the Light of the World after all.

In the Soviet Union the intellectual would belong to a privileged group: he'd be in the Writers' Union, have access to potted grouse and other delicacies, own a car, perhaps a dacha in the country. In the United States, on the other hand, he'd be treated just like anyone else. This the Marxist intellectual cannot stomach. In his vision of things he is one of the Elect and deserves the best, or at least second best. One day when there's Government by the Saints he'll come into his own. Only America stands in the way of his dream.

But, surely, with the rejection of Communism throughout Eastern Europe the intellectual has begun to reconsider? Not at all, if you know anything about the psychology of the true believer. The Marxist-Leninist will be convinced more than ever of the infallibility of the dogma. So what if it never works, if life under Communism is a bureaucratic hell and there's no food or clothing in the shops. Whatever goes wrong is not the fault of the dogma but its fallible human practitioners.

Nothing is believed in as truly as a dogma that doesn't work. This only proves how perfect it is. *Credo quia absurdum est.*

"When you talk about America in your poems it reminds me of the starch laundries put in shirts for stiffener." The speaker was one of the New York Poets. He wore a perpetual sneer; a reviewer had called his poems snotty, and I could see why. I told him I didn't think much of his idea of poetry, making jokes, and we parted with mutual detestation.

Was it true? Were the poems I had written about America worked up?

When I was seven my mother left Jamaica and went to live in Toronto. Then she lived in New York. When my brother and I were growing up we saw her only when she came to the island on brief visits. She sent us books and small gifts from America. The word America evoked her handwriting . . . it meant love and all the things the books she sent talked about. It was the world of Tom Sawyer and Huckleberry Finn, of Penrod and Sam.

Then there were the movies. For people who live in out-of-the-way places, movies are everything life is not, exciting and romantic. At school there was an old projector that had to be cranked and two films without sound. One was an eighteenth-century play, *The School for Scandal*; the actors wore wigs and the subtitles were unreadable. The other was the second Dempsey-Tunney fight, the controversial "fourteen count." The film kept breaking. We waited in the dark steamy room where laundry was ironed. The cranking would start again, the figures flickering on the bed-sheet that was used as a screen. Dempsey caught Tunney against the ropes and Tunney went down, and the film broke again.

In the vacations we went to the movies. Those of us who lived in Kingston were particularly blessed: there was the Movie Theatre at Cross Roads, and the Palace and Gaiety downtown. Some of the movies that came to the island were British but most were American: *Beau Geste, The Dawn Patrol, King Kong,* Fred Astaire and Ginger Rogers singing and dancing.

> Fair seed-time had my soul, and I grew up
> Fostered alike by beauty and by fear . . .

In the late thirties the Carib Theater opened at Cross Roads. It was very modern: the screen lit up like a rainbow, music swelled and curtains parted when the show was about to begin.

The movies made me want to go to America. And, in fact, they have made the whole world want to go to America, an America that exists only in the movies.

When I was seventeen I came to the States. Everything I saw was different and exciting: the great buildings, the men and women walking with such urgency, the lights at dusk. A New York Poet would take such things for granted, but to this day I have retained that sense of difference and excitement. I am still a stranger in America.

❧

I had no wish to go back, and as the years went by it seemed that I never would.

At school in the evening, after dinner and before Prep, the boys used to stroll to and fro on the barbecue. This was a concrete covered square the school was built around. We walked in twos or threes talking to our friends. Most often I walked with Peter Lopez. With Peter I talked about trains, boxing, and Gloria Roberts. She lived in Kingston and I had once introduced him to her. She seemed incredibly beautiful to me and, in proportion as she was beautiful, unattainable.

Sometimes I walked the barbecue with Beverly Dodd who was as avid a reader as I. We discussed *The Scarlet Pimpernel* and other adventure stories, or funny stories by W. W. Jacobs and P. G. Wodehouse. We read to be entertained. Between fifteen and sixteen, however, my tastes changed. Reading was no longer an amusement, it had become serious. I was becoming a writer, and the ways of this were to be brooded over in secret and not discussed with anyone.

You walked from the main building to Long Wall and back until the bell rang for Prep. Sometimes Patoo, the Owl, a dwarfish mulatto whose task it was to pull on the bell rope, was late in doing so, and in the few extra minutes of freedom a murmur rose from the barbecue. There was an air of happiness and excitement, a sense of what it would be like to be free. But then, inevitably, the bell would toll, and we'd go to the room where, for an hour and a half, we bent over our desks reading and writing. A Sixth Form boy sat at the front of the room to keep order. A master would look in to see that order was being maintained. The sportsmaster, Mister Dunleavy, liked to prowl on tennis shoes with a cane under his arm.

If the prefect were one we didn't respect, and the coast seemed clear, a small riot might ensue. Someone would shoot with a rubber band at the neck of a boy in front. Johnny Forsyth jumped up from his desk and brayed like a jackass, "Hee haw, hee haw!" He was holding his cock and waving it up and down. "Ah cyan't read an ah cyan't write but ah cyan multiply!" This got a laugh though it was an old joke—we had all seen Johnny's cock-stands.

One evening before Prep I was standing alone at the wall. The sun had gone down and the plain and sea beyond were growing dark. Over to the west at Black River there were two or three lights. I became aware of someone standing a few feet away. I'd been lost in thought . . . *The Return of the Native* or the battle of Waterloo . . . and hadn't seen him appear. He was a stranger, and this was remarkable. Very few visitors ever came to Munro: it was a long drive from the nearest town, then a drive up a mountain with dizzying turns.

The sportsmaster, Mister Dunleavy, appeared, heading for the infirmary. He was the lover of the school nurse and every night paid a visit to the infirmary. He also hung around the dormitories when a certain young "colored" woman was working there, one of the servants who emptied the chamberpots, made the beds, refilled the water jugs, and scrubbed the floor. They were invisible . . . we didn't see them as human beings, But this young woman was beautiful, slender and doe-eyed. She was as beautiful as Tondelayo in the movie. Johnny Forsyth, who would have liked to multiply, had his eye on her. It was a question which would get to her first, Johnny or the sportsmaster.

The stranger turned to me and spoke. "Wasn't that Dunleavy?" I said that it was. He said, "I remember him. He'd played football for a team in England. He was famous . . . he showed us his clippings: 'Dunleavy Scores Again.' He was a real star."

The last phrase marked the speaker for an American, but not exactly. His speech had traces of a British accent.

He said, "How long have you been at Munro?"

I told him. He said, "Then you'll soon be leaving. What do you plan to do?"

We talked some more. He wanted to know where I lived. I told him that we lived near Bournemouth Bath and I swam there every day during the holidays. On Saturdays and Sundays crowds of people came and a lot of tourists. I told him how silly the tourists looked, the way they dressed. When you saw them in Kingston they were buying a lot of silly stuff and spending a lot of money. They seemed very silly to me.

He said, "What about the people selling them all those silly things? Isn't there anything wrong with that?"

It was an idea that hadn't occurred to me. I had the clear views of one who lived on an island: the way we thought was the only way to think. But I seem to recall admitting that he had a point. Then the bell rang for Prep and I left.

Who was the visitor in the twilight who had come all the way from America? I think he was the one I am now, writing this.

Property and
Other Values

The cove is a meeting place for seagulls, ducks, geese, and swans. Occasionally there is a cormorant like a bird with a long neck in a Chinese painting. The cove opens on a small harbor. Most of the year it's quiet; in the summer motorboats make a racket and the shore is littered.

As you round Tinker Bluff where patriots are said to have fired on British warships, the larger harbor that gives the town its name opens before you: high ground to the east and west and the town in the valley between. All the services of a small town: a ferry, restaurants, gift shops, news agent, church, pizzeria, clothing store, supermarket, lawyer, automobile showroom, free library, tax assessor, optometrist, bank, are situated in four blocks next to the water. On the high ground to the east overlooking the town there is a large yellow building . . . St. Charles Hospital. On the west side of the harbor three chimneys, two tall and slender, one shorter by a head and shoulders, thrust up in the air . . . the Long Island Lighting Company. It can be seen for miles around. The Lighting Company is the biggest industry in Port Jefferson. Thanks to the taxes it pays, taxes on private property are low in the neighborhood. The residents appreciate this greatly: property and taxes are their main concern.

As you continue along the beach you pass Washington Park

with its benches and trash containers. Every summer the mayor of our village sends out a notice:

ANNUAL FAMILY PICNIC
Aug. 19 (rain date Aug. 20)
Burgers. Hotdogs. Salads.
Watermelon
$5.⁰⁰ per person $18 max. per household
Beer Extra. B. Y. O. B.

The notice says there will be a Biathlon (see flyer) and Kids' Games (3 Leg, Water Balloon, Wheelbarrow, Sack). Adult Eggtoss LAST. At 5:00 there will be Food & Goodies, and AFTER, Music and Dancing.

You can either retrace your steps or turn off the beach and go back through the woods. There used to be a large wooded area. That was before the man who owned the land decided to sell it to a developer. The developer submitted his plan to the county, and it was rejected; it would mean the destruction of plant and animal life. But the village can make its own laws, and the mayor and council gave the developer the go-ahead. "Moving right along," says the mayor.

I used to walk in the woods on paths overgrown with thorns and branches. There were places where you had to cut your way through, like a tropical forest. Then you came into a clearing and stood listening to the wind in the leaves.

One day when I came to the clearing two men were there, having a conversation. One I knew, the man who owned the property, we had met on social occasions. The other was a stranger in a blue suit; he had sideburns and wore dark glasses. The landowner introduced me . . . Sideburns was the developer. They continued their conversation . . . about building houses. I said, "You're not building them here!" They turned and looked at me. "We're not?"

Construction was to start on Monday, and has been going on ever since: the clanking of bulldozers, the scream of a tree being fed to the machine that turns a tree into wood chips. On our walks Miriam and I have seen the houses in all stages of construction. A day to pour the foundation, two weeks to put up the frame. The wood is of the cheapest kind . . . it splits when a nail is driven. There are only a few inches between the inner and outer walls. Put in plumbing and electricity and a heating system, attach windows and doors, and *voila!*, a house that sells for four hundred thousand dollars.

The design is Barbie and Ken, stamped out of plastic. Then there are what the developer calls "manor" houses, large boxlike structures that stand on their one acre like an elephant on a pea patch.

The woods have been cut down and the animals driven out. Traffic on the roads has doubled. The roadsides are littered with beer cans and glass, and the stones on the shore have turned black.

We know two carpenters, a married couple, who are building these houses . . . two of the friendliest people you'll ever meet, and it's good to see them working side by side, husband and wife, sawing and hammering. Besides, they like our dogs . . . they have one of their own. On our walks we stop to talk to them. I tell them they're destroying the world. When they drive by in their van on the way home he waves and shouts that they've finished their destroying for the day.

Can you blame a carpenter for practicing his trade? People need houses, and if they are willing to pay four hundred thousand for a house with thin walls and a basement that floods when it rains, that's their privilege. But was it necessary to cut down the whole forest? Couldn't a part have been saved for future generations?

I met the landowner at the house of a mutual friend. He said that his family had owned the land as far back as anyone could remember, and talked about the so-called ecologists who had tried to prevent him from selling it. He had a pale complexion that reddened with anger as he spoke. It was his property and he could do with it as he pleased.

He didn't give a damn for the future generations. What had they ever done for him, he wanted to know.

Some of the residents appear to be quite mad. One day when we were walking below the tideline, where everyone has a right to walk, it's the law, a stout man with white whiskers and a red face came shouting toward us, telling us to get off his property. I asked him how far he thought his property extended . . . he must know, only to the tideline. He said that this was arguable, and he said in a loud voice, "King's rights!" He was invoking a law that obtained in the eighteenth century, in the reign of King George, that gave people who owned a part of the shoreline rights to the land in front of it as well, at the bottom of the sea.

Some residents try to enlarge their property by encroaching on their neighbor's or on public land. This is done stealthily, by feet and inches. There are no sidewalks, but the ground next to the road, where a sidewalk would be, belongs to the village. One woman has extended her lawn right down to the road and placed large rocks in a line, a foot in from the road. She hopes by so doing to establish a claim to the strip running next to the road.

I thought it far-fetched when I read in *Dead Souls* about Chichikov's playing chess with a man who tried to cheat him by moving the chessmen when he thought Chichikov wasn't looking. How could anyone cheat at chess? But was this more far-fetched than what this woman is doing, coming down at night with another large rock in a wheelbarrow, to place it beside the road? Some day she'll have established her claim to the strip of ground. I think the statute says seven years . . . if no one challenges your claim to a piece of land for seven years, it's yours to have and to hold.

Until death do you part. But this woman will shout from the grave that the ground next to the road belongs to her and no one else may walk on it.

All they seem to care about is property. And what's the alternative? The state owning the land and doling it out . . . to the deserving. The police state with its spies and informers . . . those who serve the state having what they want, the rest waiting in line. Who would want to live in such a world? Some would: they see themselves sitting among the rulers, telling others what to think.

"I'm an intellectual," one of them told me recently.

Every now and then a magazine editor thinks that it's time for an article on "contemporary poetry" and someone is foolish enough to write it. Poetry, he tells us, is in a very bad way in the United States. Why? Because only a few hundred people will buy a book of poems, whereas in 1810 *The Lady of the Lake* was immensely popular. Or else he tells us that poetry is flourishing because there are lots of poetry readings.

These people aren't talking about poetry but something else. They would like poetry to be like the ANNUAL FAMILY PICNIC. Burgers. Hotdogs. Salads. Watermelon. They see poets competing in the Biathlon, 3-Leg, and Water Balloon. Prizes will be given, and AFTER there will be Music and Dancing.

But poetry is written out of the need one has to write it. There is a void in oneself that echoes the Void without. I think Leonardo, and more recently a Surrealist, said that they stared at a wall until shapes began to form. If you look long enough into the void, sounds are heard and shapes begin to appear.

This morning as I stared at the grass, leaves, and "a sky empty and void of ideas," a wedding was taking place. It actually happened a year ago: the son of a friend was being married. Our friend, the mother of the groom, had made bouquets of artificial flowers for the bride and bridesmaids, and she had also gone to considerable trouble making parasols for the bridesmaids to carry.

These people were Pentecostal Christians. If such were typical of the "working class," the intellectual might consider them worthy. But many so-called ordinary people aren't at all typical . . . they have their own ideas.

Our poets, also, don't find them worthy, for they seem to be enjoying themselves. Our poets are not interested in other people, especially if they seem to be having a good time.

The wedding was to take place on a stage at the end of the church. This was decorated with a green arch with letters of gold . . . "Jesus Is Savior." There were baskets of artificial flowers . . . had Samantha made those too? There were several microphones. On the left side of the stage, that is, to our left as we faced it, there was a choir with a synthesizer and electric guitar. On the right side, an orchestra with a baby grand.

The synthesizer played the Wedding March and the bride and groom came down the aisle. She wore a white gown; her train was carried by two children, a boy and girl dressed in white. There followed half a dozen bridesmaids in gowns of various colors: lavender, peach, pink, blue, green, and yellow. Each young woman was wearing a picture hat and carrying a bouquet and parasol, and each was accompanied by a young man.

> Uncle Bob prayed over the groom:
> "Let him establish Kingdom principles."
> Aunt Shirley prayed for the bride:
> "Father, I pray an anointing on her."
> "Love," said Reverend Phillips,
>
> "is insensitive, love is invalueless."
> He said that we merger together
> in holy matrimony,
> and the choir burst into song:
> "He waits for us, and waits for us."

> Every day they went swimming in the pool
> and rode the two water scooters.
> They rented two deck chairs
> and sat on the sand in the sun.
> A breeze made the palm leaves whisper.

The sea is green close to shore,
further out it is blue.
The ship standing still on the horizon
makes you think of sailing away
forever with the one you love.

Jennifer ordered the roast beef platter,
Mike had the fish cakes.
"I thought you didn't like fish,"
she said. "Well," he said, "I guess you were wrong."
Tears came to her eyes. The honeymoon was over.

But then they went to their room
and everything was OK.
In the evening they went dancing
and stayed up late on the veranda
looking at the lights and the moon.

And you, *hypocrite lecteur,*
what makes you so superior?

Jimmy

It could not have been easy for Jimmy Ernst to think about his famous father, Max, with any degree of objectivity. When Jimmy was two, Max left his wife and child and went to live in Paris. In his autobiography Jimmy suggests that a perfectly natural and innocent reaction on his part may have influenced Max to abandon his wife and infant son.

A number of Dadaist poets and artists were spending the summer in some old buildings on a farm near Tarranz in the Austrian Alps. They were Max Ernst, his wife Louise, and Jimmy: the poet Paul Eluard and his wife Gala; the poet Tristan Tzara, and the sculptor Hans Arp. There were visitors such as the American writer Matthew Josephson and his wife. One day everyone went swimming in the nude. Jimmy's mother was holding him when the surface broke and Max came up laughing and holding out his arms. Lou was lifting Jimmy toward his father when Jimmy saw innumerable long-legged water-skating insects on the glassy surface surrounding Max's body. He began to scream and struggled against being handed over. "Max's face went dark and angry; he turned and swam away." That same day Max told Lou that he was leaving to join Gala and Paul in Paris. There Max, Gala, and Paul lived in a ménage à trois.

Lou continued to live in Cologne where she earned a living as an art critic. She lived freely as a single woman "in a society that had a very low opinion of such an existence," and she seems not to have held a grievance against Max. He was an unusual man, she would say, whose work was more important to him than the ordinary rules of behavior. "They had loved each other very much." But Jimmy was not so forgiving . . . for the first seventeen years of his life he would say that he wanted to have nothing to do with art. "Lou-Straus endured many a teenage diatribe from her son against an absent father." She said, "Maybe you will feel differently when you grow up."

Twice a year Jimmy traveled to Paris to see Max Ernst. There he met the Surrealists, their wives and mistresses. Gala had left Paul Eluard and married Salvador Dali. The list of Max's friends and acquaintances reads like a roll call of the avant-garde. There are some paintings by Jimmy Ernst of Kachina Indians dancing with masks and rattles beneath a sky filled with whirling lights. Those Indians, it seems to me, are really Max and his friends.

> A line of masked dancers
> facing you, their eyes are slits . . .
> holding rattles in their hands,
> the sky behind them on fire . . .
> Max Ernst and Paul Eluard,
> Giacometti, Man Ray, Miró,
> Soupault . . . all the Surrealists
> lighting up the sky of Paris . . .
> all the Kachina Indians!

In Germany things were becoming more and more difficult. Lou-Straus Ernst could no longer sell her articles, for she was a Jew. In 1933 she moved to Paris, leaving Jimmy in the care of her family. Jimmy saw the rise of the Nazis and how they treated Jews.

I had shaken with terror and fury at the sight of bearded Hasidim, their women and children, on their knees, scrubbing sidewalks on a Sabbath surrounded by roaring Brownshirts and giggling burghers of Cologne. . . . I had seen a marching troop of Hitler Youth suddenly breaking rank, overturning and setting fire to the newspaper kiosk of a blind Jew; the smashing of synagogue and church windows in full daylight as traffic and commerce continued at their usual pace and nearby policemen watched with amusement.

Jimmy's parents arranged for him to leave Germany and go to the United States. When France went to war with Germany, Max Ernst was interned in Aix-en-Provence with others who were technically still German. Lou Straus was interned, then released. Jimmy and Peggy Guggenheim managed to have Max brought to America. Peggy Guggenheim intended to marry Max and she enlisted the help of some very important people. Jimmy lists them: Nelson Rockefeller, John Hay Whitney, American Smelting and Refining, the Borough President of Manhattan, Edward M. Warburg, people from the Morgan Bank, Lehman Brothers, and Eleanor Roosevelt.

Max Ernst was a famous artist but Lou Straus-Ernst was only an art historian, so no one vouched for her. The French handed her over to the Germans—the French were more than willing to hand Jews over to the Germans. Lou Straus-Ernst's destination was Auschwitz, where she was gassed.

> At Auschwitz shortly before the end
> one had seen her: "A woman totally exhausted,
> half lying, half leaning against a wall,
> warming herself in the last rays of a dying sun."

I don't know how Jimmy managed to live with that knowledge, but he did. Once he showed me a page with a printed list of names. The Jews were sent from Paris in box cars. The French carefully recorded the name of every Jew and the railroad car in which he or she was transported to a concentration camp. Jimmy showed me the name of his mother . . . there it was, Lou-Straus Ernst, and the number of the railroad car.

> And still we believe in loving-kindness . . .
> some even believe there's a God.
> This is a mystery, *ein Rätsel*
> God himself could not explain.

✤

Jimmy lived in East Hampton where the waves come rolling from the Old World. The houses set well back from the street are modeled on English manor houses and French chateaus. In a cemetery off the main street there's a tomb with the effigy of a knight in armor, as pleased to be there as though he were lying in a churchyard in Kent.

East Hampton attracted artists and many who liked the noise of art. They went to the gallery showings where they might meet a celebrity and touch the hem of his or her garment. They managed to get onto people's lawns and into their houses. Jimmy and Dallas Ernst held receptions to which artists and writers came, and many who were not invited. They stood on the lawn consuming drinks and canapés. There would be two or three celebrities. Kurt Vonnegut reclined in a deck chair. The name evoked Kurtz in *Heart of Darkness*, and he had the same elongated, bony frame as Kurtz lying on a litter. Like Kurtz he had a devoted following . . . young people swore by his novels. And there by the pool was Betty Friedan who wrote *The Feminine Mystique*.

I was there because Jimmy was painting a picture based on one of my poems. It had been Lillian Braude's idea to bring painters and poets together and have them make paintings that were based on poetry or actually incorporated lines. I don't know how it worked for others, but the project had been a godsend for Jimmy and me. Unlike most painters, Jimmy was a reader—he had studied in a gymnasium in Cologne, and when he came to the States he read the poems of Yeats . . . in order to improve his English! He also read *Studs Lonigan* in order to understand the New World.

He read all the poems I sent him, and they seemed to mean as much to him as to me. I was moved by his enthusiasm . . . poetry isn't everyone's cup of tea. I had been going through a period of doubt . . . why should you keep on writing verse when no one seemed to care? If all the poets in the United States stopped writing, would anyone notice? Jimmy's feeling for my poems gave me a tremendous lift. For the first time in years I felt that my poems might really mean something to others, that the ideas they expressed might not be just my own but real. For they meant so much to Jimmy.

One poem of mine he particularly like was "To the Western World." It was written in meter and rhyme, a form I no longer used, but the feeling still held. The poem must have spoken to Jimmy of an idea he'd had himself. That is the writing that moves us, not someone's attempt to express an idea no one else has had, in a way no one else would say it. The writing that matters speaks to our common humanity in words that everyone can understand.

Jimmy was a stranger in America as I was, and he wanted to understand his adoptive country. What made the New World different from the Old? What did it mean to be an American? I think that Jimmy felt he was breaking new ground with his painting, and I have felt it about my writing. This feeling was what the poem, "To the Western World," expressed.

Jimmy's paintings, the ones you saw when you went into the house, were like the patterns in a kaleidoscope. I suppose if you had a father who made you think of water bugs, if you saw Surrealist paintings when you were growing up, and the way the Surrealists carried on, and if you saw the Nazis marching and beating up people in the street, you would want to inhabit a world of rectangles and circles, colors as bright as the colors of Eden. You would want regularity.

The painting Jimmy was doing based on one of my poems was different. A shape exploded upward across the canvas like a bird. There was a caged bird in the poem . . . I was speaking of the habit of not expressing your thought directly but in a metaphor. This must have struck a chord in Jimmy, one that wanted to be free, not to express his feelings in a pattern but directly. Lines of the poem marched across the canvas in block capitals like a cage, and behind them were those exploding wings.

ON WINTER NIGHTS WHEN THE MOON
HUNG STILL BEHIND SOME SCAFFOLDING
YOU THOUGHT, "LIKE A BIRD IN A CAGE."
YOU WERE ALWAYS MAKING COMPARISONS . . .
"FINDING SIMILITUDES IN DISSIMILARS,"
SAYS ARISTOTLE. A FORM OF INSANITY . . .
NOTHING IS EVER WHAT IT APPEARS TO BE,
BUT ALWAYS LIKE SOMETHING ELSE.

We were going to do great things together . . . publish a book of his drawings and my poems. He walked around the studio wiping his hands on a rag, a stocky man with a round face and light blue eyes. He was bald on top as I was. There was something elfish about Jimmy's appearance.

Baldness wasn't all we had in common. there was a Jewish mother and Gentile father, and growing up, in my case, not knowing that you were a Jew, and in Jimmy's case not caring . . . he had grown up, as many German Jews did, believing that he was like everyone else, *echt Deutsch.*

But why look for reasons? You either like someone or you don't. At a time in life when old friends fall away and you don't make new ones, I had found a brother.

He was writing a story of his life and he let me see the manuscript. I made some corrections of the style but it was strong and flowing. And he was painting with a new freedom and strength. I don't think there was ever a happier man than Jimmy in those months. He had come to terms with his famous father . . . he had gone around him and found a way of painting of his own. He didn't have to fall short of Max Ernst, or go beyond him, he could go around.

He would never come to terms with his mother's death. How could he? The world will never be able to accept the Holocaust. Only God could explain it, and a God who explained it would be one you wouldn't want to know.

Jimmy and Dallas had a place in Florida where they stayed

during the winter months. He came up to New York to see his book launched and hold an exhibition of new paintings. He was hanging them in the gallery when he collapsed and died. He had had a heart bypass operation some years before. The effort of hanging paintings, and the excitement, killed him.

Among Jimmy's papers Dallas found the poem, "To the Western World," of which he had been so fond. She asked me to read it over his grave.

> The treasures of Cathay were never found.
> In this America, this wilderness
> Where the axe echoes with a lonely sound,
> The generations labor to possess
> And grave by grave we civilize the ground.

The Memorial
and the Garden

I got out of bed, dressed, and put on my socks and boots . . . carefully, for my feet hurt. Then I wrote myself a pass and made my way to the outer door. The corporal on duty looked at the piece of paper and looked at me, then he waved me through. A decent corporal.

I must have limped for miles, making a round of the bars. For years after the war I would dream I was walking in Paris in streets that were growing dark. I had to be back by nightfall. Just one more street, one more bar, before I'd have to go.

How long was I in that hospital? I don't remember, but it wasn't long. Those of us who weren't basket cases were needed at the front. I remember thinking that it would be rotten luck to be killed just as I was starting to know Paris and the war would soon be over.

We are staying at a hotel on the Left Bank five blocks east of Boulevard Saint Michel and a block south of Saint Germain: bed, bath and breakfast for 380 francs or $67, the price subject to change but still a bargain compared with Right Bank prices. A friend of ours, Margaret Lally, pays twice as much for a room on the Right Bank near Gare St. Lazare. We have an open air market down the street from our hotel, and a laundry. There are a number of inexpensive restaurants. In the brasserie with a green front at the top of rue des Carmes you can have a very good lunch, "Formule Express," for 59 francs, wine and coffee extra. My concern with hotel prices, laundry, and restaurants may seem excessive, but travelers have to think about such things. First the stomach, then the museum or whatever it is that strikes your fancy.

This morning we walked to Sainte-Chapelle, crossing the Ile de la Cité. At the entrance to the courtyard I was stopped by a gendarme who wanted to see my passport. I'd left it back at the hotel but I showed him an American Express credit card and this seemed to allay his suspicions—apparently the person he was looking for didn't use credit cards. He showed me a police circular with a picture of a man with hooded eyes and a three-day growth of beard, to whom, he said, I bore a resemblance. "Well," I said, "but I shave."

Miriam had been watching the proceedings at a distance. When I rejoined her and we were standing in line to buy tickets she kept looking at me as though I were up to something. I said that I liked the idea of being taken for a dangerous criminal and that if I played my hand right I might find myself in jail gaining new experiences. How would she like that? She said that she wouldn't like it at all.

We walked around the chapel looking at the stained glass and comparing scenes with the descriptions in our guide book. Above one alcove there was a panel showing Jesus with small angels to each side, hands pressed together in adoration, ascending toward him on a curve. I made a sketch of this. I remarked to Miriam that Jews, most Jews, knew nothing of Christianity and the civilization that built Sainte-Chapelle, for they didn't accept Jesus as the Messiah.

From the book she had been reading, Chaim Potok's *My Name*

is Asher Lev, she gathered that according to the Hasidim the proof
that Jesus was not the Messiah was all the terrible things that had
happened to Jews over the years. If Jesus had been the Messiah he
would not have permitted these things to happen.

I have many ideas on the subject of Christians and Jews, for I
was brought up as a Christian and then, when I came to America,
discovered that my mother was Jewish. One of my ideas is that if
Jesus was not the Messiah at the time of the Crucifixion, he
became the Messiah in the two thousand years after: belief made
him so. Another idea I have is that God has abandoned the world
—not only the God of the Jews but the God of the Christians too.
As the poet says,

> The voice of Rachel mourning for her loss
> Rose from the German death camps every day.
> In silence Christ descended from the cross
> And went, without a parable, away.

After leaving the chapel we walked in the direction of the
Seine. There was a sign, "To the Monument of the Deportation."
I told Miriam that I wanted very much to see it. I was thinking of
my friend Jimmy Ernst whose mother had been handed over by
the French to the Germans, who took her to Auschwitz and killed
her there.

We asked a gendarme directions to the monument and he
pointed us to Notre Dame Cathedral. We walked towards it and
again asked a gendarme directions. This was a young gendarme.
He became thoughtful. He drew a book out of a pocket and turned
the pages. It became obvious that he didn't have the first idea how
to use it. We thanked him for his trouble and walked on. "I could
have found it in seconds," Miriam said. True, she's an expert in
research, but could you take his book from a gendarme and embar-
rass him?

At the cathedral no monument to the deportation and no sign
. . . We asked a passing Frenchman and he directed us to the
Hôtel de Ville. From there, he said, we should ask directions . . .
it was too complicated to explain.

We arrived at the Hôtel de Ville to find the main entrance
blocked by scaffolding. Inquiries brought us to another entrance,
at the rear of the building, and a window marked "Information,"
with two women who were indifferent about providing any. One
of them remarked that there had been many deportations. I said
in a loud voice, "For the Jews. Who are dead."

This had an effect. One of them made a telephone call, then
handed me a slip of paper with the address of an office of "cultural affairs." We'd have to go there if we wanted information. It
was a considerable distance away. It seemed that the deportation
of Jews was a well-kept secret—if there was a monument you
couldn't find it.

A man was standing near us looking at a bulletin board and
making notes. He asked what we were looking for. He said, "That
is only for Jews who were deported." Yes, I said, that was what
we wanted to see. "It is not a monument," he said, "but 'The
Memorial to the Unknown Jewish Martyr.'" He seemed very concerned that we should not be misled. I assured him that we would
like to see the memorial. Very well, he was going in that direction
and would show us the way.

I asked him who he was. Did he work at the Hôtel de Ville?
No. He was a man who lived here. He was born in Paris.

I said that we had been unable to find the monument or
anyone who could tell us where it was. He said there was a reason
. . . it was a matter of "security."

I thought he would go with us part way, give us directions, and
leave, but he stayed with us through streets and turnings until
we arrived. It wasn't a monument but a museum, and a sign
on the door said that it was closed from 12 to 2 . . . right now, in
fact. This didn't faze our guide: he spoke to an elderly woman
who was just leaving, and she unlocked the door and admitted us.
He asked if it would disturb us if he came with us, and I said that
it wouldn't. Not only did he come with us, he insisted on buying
our tickets.

There were three floors of photographs showing the history of
European Jewry from the invasion of Poland to the founding of a

Jewish state: photographs of Jews being beaten or shot or herded to the gas chamber. There were mounds of naked bodies.

There were also texts: for example, a chart showing rations and prices posted by the Germans.

Number of calories:

Germans	2310
Foreigners	1790
Poles	634
Jews	184

The Jews were made to pay an exorbitant sum for their wretched portion.

There were photographs of individuals and groups that had fought in the resistance. A photograph of a bearded man named Janusz Korckzak, "writer and eminent pedagogue" . . . Our guide said that this man ran a camp for children. When they were taken by the Germans he went with them to the gas chamber.

We were on the floor devoted to France under the occupation. He said that at the trial of Klaus Barbie, two years ago, the full extent of the collaboration of the French with the Nazis had been revealed for the first time. The Pétain government—in fact, the French people—gave the Germans more than they asked for. The Germans wanted Jews who were sixteen and older. The French gave them the Jewish children also.

He asked who we were, and was amused when I said that I came from Jamaica in the West Indies. How did I happen to be there? I said that my father wasn't Jewish but my mother was; she came from Russia and many of her relatives had been killed by the Germans. I told him I was here in Paris during the war as a soldier. An expression of puzzlement or alarm crossed his face. In the American army, I assured him.

I said that Miriam's background was Jewish. As a young girl she had been a Zionist: she went to Israel and joined a kibbutz.

He said that he wasn't religious. Many Jews in France were not, for how could you believe in God after this? There were Jews who kept up Jewish customs and traditions but were not religious.

He led the way downstairs to a room below street level. There was a concrete Star of David set in the floor with a flame burning in the middle. He put on a yarmulke and asked me to cover my head . . . this was a religious place. We stood for a while in silence. There was writing in Hebrew on the wall, but none of us could read it.

He said that every year on July the 16th a "rafle" or roundup of Jews was held at Place Bir-Hakeim. Bir-Hakeim used to be a stadium for bicycle racing. The French police brought the Jews there in order to hand them over to the Germans. The building was no longer standing but every year there was "La Rafle" to commemorate the event, attended by the President of France and representatives of foreign governments. Following the ceremony they came her to honor the dead.

We said goodbye outside the building. He asked what I did, and I said I was a writer, which seemed to please him greatly. We exchanged addresses: I wrote ours on a sheet of note paper and he gave us his card.

After we'd parted from him we looked at it. He was *Secrétaire Général* of the *Fédération des Societés Juives de France*.

This was the man who appeared when we were about to give up our search for the monument . . . the secretary of Jewish societies in France. What were the chances of our meeting? In the old days they would have said that he was a messenger sent by God.

Coda: In the Garden of Plants

We went to the Jardin des Plantes and sat on a bench that faced the flower beds, eating bread and cheese and drinking wine.

Two old ladies came by, leaning against each other, talking. Pals.

Then a group of six-year-olds with two adults in charge. Are children the answer to those of whom our guide spoke, those who no longer believe in God? Is God reborn in each generation?

We walked among tea roses:

Quebec Mme. Marie Curie A. A. R. S. 1944
Hyb. Thé Gaujard 1943
Michele Meilland Hyb. Thé F. Meilland 1945

They were giving prizes for tea roses during the war, at the same time that they were sending children to be killed. What kind of people were these?

Among the flower beds a little girl stood holding a pink cloud of sugar on a stick. She licked the cloud then tore off a piece and ate it. We stood and watched for a while. It was sheer happiness to watch her.

4

The Vigil

Rosalind smiled when she saw us. She seems to be aware of what is happening, and can understand what you say if you speak in a loud voice. But she cannot speak, only utter sounds when she needs something or is in pain. She stopped talking some months ago and the vocal cords have deteriorated, as have the muscles of her arms and legs. She can neither move nor speak.

I said that everyone sent their love and Herbert had recovered completely. This was not exactly true: my brother had a heart attack; the doctor recommended surgery but he wouldn't have it— he said that he could cure himself with proper diet and exercise.

I told her that Miriam and I thought about her constantly and I had been writing about her, how she stood outside the church where they were singing "Jesus Christ is risen." How she went up to the roof where her grandmother kept tomatoes and cucumbers and brought some down to share with the other children.

Later Miriam and I went for a walk on Viale Carducci. She said that it was good to talk to Rosalind in this way about the past.

I haven't told my mother everything I've written about her— some of the things I said wouldn't have pleased her at all. I never showed her the book in which I wrote about our life in Jamaica. My writing used to puzzle her and make her uneasy. She remarked of one poem, "Typhus," in which I wrote about the death of her sister Lisa, that I wrote about things that didn't make you feel happy.

Vincenza says that Rosalind's life is drawing to a close: she may not last beyond the New Year. Renato says, "La poverina . . . Rosalind è finita." What will he do when she's gone? His life has been bound up with hers for thirty-five years. It has been exhausting to take care of her, and at times he has been driven almost crazy with worry, but when she's no longer here his life will have no purpose.

She is never left unattended; she has a great fear of being left alone; her eyes follow you about the room. Though she cannot speak she seems to understand when Vincenza, speaking close to her ear in a low voice, asks, "Where does it hurt? Is it your leg? Your arm?" She tries to answer but only makes noises. But Vincenza understands and places ointment on a hand and massages it gently.

Vincenza is the trained nurse. In the morning when the housekeeper, Grazia, has given Rosalind her breakfast, Vincenza arrives. There is also a male nurse who gives Rosalind her bath and an enema if one is needed. At two in the afternoon Vincenza leaves and a young woman named Alessandra takes her place. She knows how to perform simple tasks: changing Rosalind's position in bed or on the chair, giving her medicine or something to drink. When Alessandra leaves, Grazia gives Rosalind her evening meal and stays in the room for an hour. Then another woman, Angela, arrives, and the male nurse returns to give Rosalind an injection so she can sleep. Angela stays with her through the night.

✦

In the evening we ate at Montecatini—we shall be taking our meals out, except breakfast. Grazia has her hands full helping in the sickroom—she cannot cook besides.

The restaurant owner, a woman of large proportions, welcomed us back with a big smile and inquired after my mother. We were also greeted by the man who waited on our table last summer. He has white hair and an expression of sensitivity and patient suffering. But the *antipasti*, a specialty of the house, were not in evidence. On our previous visits there was a table of *antipasti*: marinated shrimps, potato puffs, marinated mushrooms, salmon, fried zucchini pancakes, *calamari* in oil and vinegar, white beans with scallions . . . twenty dishes to choose from, and these were only the first course, the *antipasti*!

The waiter said that there was no "movement," so it didn't pay to have the *antipasti*, they would only have to be thrown out. "No movement" gave us to understand that the failure of customers to appear was due to a physical law, not some fault of the restaurant.

The proprietor said that it was because of the World Cup—everyone was watching football on television. and this, she said, rolling her eyes to heaven, would continue until July the 8th.

The proprietor and the waiter commiserated with us on the performance of the American team against Czechoslovakia. The Czech team wasn't one of the best, yet the score was Czechoslovakia 5, U.S. 1. They wondered if America would ever take to football. I said I didn't think so: young people didn't grow up playing it. Tomorrow the Americans were playing Italy, one of the best teams in the tournament: the outcome didn't bear thinking of.

When we left the restaurant we saw that the proprietor had put up a sign, "Sala TV," hoping to attract customers.

We walked back on Viale Carducci. At the Piazza Mazzini a large TV screen had been erected and a crowd was watching the game. Argentina was ahead of Russia, 1-0, and the Russians were fouling like crazy, tripping the Argentinean forwards. A line of young Italians sitting on the curb in front of us were distressed every time the referee blew his whistle and gave the Argentineans a penalty kick. Fans of the Soviet Union. "What's there to like about Russia?" Miriam remarked.

Today is Thursday when there's an open-air market and people come from all directions to buy clothing, shoes, kitchen utensils, toys, meat and produce, at bargain prices. We walked around the market, then went to the beach and ate lunch at Lidino. We are regular customers and on friendly terms with the family: Valeria and her daughter Suzanna who wait on the tables; Flavio, Valeria's husband, who makes some of the dishes; Flavio's father, who sits and talks to people or reads the newspaper, and a grandmother who does most of the cooking. They are all concerned to know what is happening at the villa across the street.

Italians want to know about you . . . about your life. They don't understand surliness . . . people who look down at the ground and not around them. It doesn't matter how successful a man is if he doesn't seem to be enjoying life. The solitary person, the one without enjoyment, is an object of pity or contempt.

When I first came to Italy I understood none of this—I was unwilling to be pleased. That year I was working on my dissertation on a Scottish author . . . a subject as far removed from Italian life as possible. I was reading about people who kept sheep on the bare hills of Scotland in the wind and rain. Or else they were cutting one another's throats. I was studying the harsh doctrine of John Knox, the idea of predestination, the gloomy view of life that divided humankind into those who were saved from birth and marked for heaven, and those who were irrevocably damned. This made for an interesting idea that my author, James Hogg, had used to good effect. What if a man knew he was saved: couldn't he then do anything—lie, steal, fornicate, commit murder—and still be assured of his place in heaven?

With matters such as this on my mind I had little time for the life around me. Other Americans at the Academy on the hill above St. Peter's made forays into Rome and came back with reports of the wonders they had seen . . . some work of art or good, cheap restaurant. They dug up bits of pottery that were said to be Etruscan. But I sat typing in an apartment that had a marble floor, blowing on my fingers to warm them.

I disliked the religion that hung over the city like smog. I agreed with Dostoievsky: he said that the Romans were like people who lived by exhibiting the corpse of their grandmother. On the other hand they seemed frivolous and empty-headed. I looked dourly on their enjoyments.

If you really want to hate people you must hate them in their pleasures: the Englishman at cricket; the German drinking beer; the Italian promenading.

Since that time, with many visits to Italy, my idea of the Italians has changed. What I took to be frivolity I now see as a wish to offset poverty, illness, and old age. Not to mention volcanic eruptions, and the wars that sweep across the land, leaving ruins. In the face of these things, the young promenade with their arms around each other, and an old man and woman go by on a two-seater bicycle, pedaling with dignity.

The women who tend my mother's sickbed, Miriam says, are angels. Their patience is incredible; they go about their tasks with affection for the sufferer. Perhaps they really are angels: there couldn't be much difference between Grazia, Vincenza, Alessandra, Angela and the beings we see depicted in paintings who inhabit a higher sphere of existence. Perhaps there is no difference at all, and a Fra Angelico, a Giotto, are saying, "Look at the faces around you."

And the land is so beautiful! At the moment I'm sitting with Miriam on the back porch. On the porch itself there are flower pots with red roses, flowers the color of fuschia, whose name we don't know, and geraniums. Cherries are hanging a few feet away—the porch is level with the boughs. There is also a tree laden with apricots. In the garden below, white, rose-colored, blue, and lavender hydrangeas . . .

The houses nearby are painted white, yellow, or sand, with red tile roofs. Two apartment buildings overlook the villa and people can see us sitting here . . . as if anyone cared. In the distance there are umbrella pines and the foliage of the park with some trees that glitter like aspens. A large white cloud stands in a blue sky. But for the cloud the Apuan Alps would be visible, blue and jagged against the lighter blue of the sky.

Miriam is reading George Gissing's *The Private Papers of Henry Ryecroft*, and on the table in front of me lies Stephen Gill's life of

Wordsworth. I can read only a few pages at a time—scholars write
a language no one uses: "Perhaps Wordsworth even ploughed
through the revised *Political Justice* and found it rebarbitive."

I plan to review the book along with the life of Coleridge by
Richard Holmes. I would like to show the difference between
Wordsworth and Coleridge's approach to poetry as a spiritual
endeavor and the way Americans go about it. In the United States
poetry is a business like any other. Writing workshops produce a
great deal of verse that is made to order—none of it really matters to anyone. This useless industry is presided over by teachers
of "creative writing" and others who make a career out of review-
ing books of poetry and awarding grants and prizes.

We read for a while then go upstairs and sit by my mother's
bed. Vincenza has to give her a massage, so I go outside. Renato
is sitting on a chair outside the door, as he often does. Sometimes
he falls asleep in the chair. Grazia is also present. Renato asks me
a question I have difficulty understanding, for he talks too fast.
Grazia interprets: she has learned how to speak to Americans,
slowly, for she has a sister who lives in the States and sometimes
comes to visit.

Renato is asking if I think that Rosalind knows. I take him to
mean, that she's dying. I say yes, I think she knows.

Renato says that he has no idea what Rosalind is thinking.

Grazia thinks that she doesn't know.

I say that Rosalind has fought hard all her life, and it's possible
that she knows and still wants to live.

Renato wishes that she didn't want to live. There are times
when she is in great pain.

I say, "Today?"

No, he says, not today.

These are the conversations you have when someone is dying.

❧

Italy beat the U.S., 1-0. Miriam and I were having dinner at La
Casina, the restaurant in the park, when the match began. We

watched part of it on TV. The Italians scored a goal after a few minutes of play and we couldn't stand it—we left. But then we watched the rest of the match with Renato in his room. He's an expert on football—his brother Giorgio was a star player—and he is fed up with the Italians. They kept missing the goal, shooting over it or to the side. He stood up and made motions of banging his head on the wall.

After the match, cars went down Viale Carducci blowing their horns, but the Italians didn't have anything to feel proud of. They have been playing international football for years, the Americans are just getting started. In the second half the Americans seemed to be getting the hang of it and came close to evening the score.

At breakfast this morning Grazia gave us another reason that the local fans aren't elated. The match took place in Naples, and the fans in Viareggio don't like the Neapolitans.

There have been "incidents," brawls, when people from Viareggio went to football matches in Naples. The people of Viareggio begrudge the Neapolitans the prestige of "hosting" a World Cup match.

We are at Antaura, the *bagno* directly across the street from the villa. This part of the beach, with its bathhouse and umbrellas and chairs, is one of several bathing establishments that the Barsantis own. From here the villa looks rather comical, three stories topped with a square tower like a hat. It seems to be standing on tiptoe, peering out to sea.

You come to a place casually and have no liking for it . . . you may even dislike it. But time passes and one day you realize that much of your life has been spent there. Your connection with the place is like Swann's with Odette: "To think that I've wasted years of my life, that I've longed to die, that I've experienced my greatest love, for a woman who didn't appeal to me, who wasn't even my type!"

Well, not quite . . . I haven't wasted years of my life in

Viareggio; it hasn't affected me so that I've wanted to die. But I've stayed here more times than I can remember, though at first glance the place didn't appeal to me.

What Swann doesn't seem to grasp is that it isn't Odette he became involved with so casually, but life. We are more at the mercy of accidents than we think we are. Hundreds of years ago people knew this very well—they wrote of Dame Fortuna with respect. But for the past two centuries, since making a god of Science, we have lived in the belief that we can control everything. And that is true: we can control everything, except our lives, and we are shocked when something happens that is out of our control.

I came to Viareggio because Rosalind and Renato had moved here. Before that they were living at San Alessio, a few minutes' drive from Lucca. Lucca was an ancient town with buildings as fine as any in Florence. There was a wall around the town that dated back to Roman times . . . so wide that there was a road on top of the wall on which cars could drive.

Rosalind and Renato bought and renovated a villa in San Alessio. The Villa Rosalinda with its surrounding acres was a showplace. The estate produced wine—Renato saw to this, he dealt with the *contadini*, the tenant farmers. That is, when he wasn't absent in Rome on some business to be done for his brother Benvenuto, "the Engineer," who lived in Venezuela. That was where the Engineer had made his fortune.

But Rosalind and Renato were growing old and they could no longer manage the estate. So they sold it and moved to Viareggio. The Villa Selene belonged to the Engineer, but he would let them use it. Some years ago Rosalind had picked it out and persuaded him to buy it and had furnished it for him.

Viareggio is just a resort town. People come here in the summer to use the beach. It isn't one of the fancy resorts but unashamedly middleclass, a family town. Once upon a time Viareggio had pretensions: cousins of royalty used to stay at the Hotel Principe di Piemonte or the Grand Hotel and Royal. But these days half the rooms are empty, or else they are filled with groups of tourists from Britain or Germany on economy tours.

The Viale Carducci, running parallel to the beach, holds nearly all of Viareggio that is worth seeing: shops that sell clothing, handbags, cigarette lighters, at fancy prices. There are dozens of hotels and pensiones. Halfway along the street is the square I've mentioned where people gather to watch football on a screen.

What else is there to say about Viareggio? They award a literary prize every year—the Viale Carducci is named after a poet, Giosuè Carducci, who flourished before the Great War and employed the sweeping oratory of the period. I think that by 1915 this must have been passing. "*Avanti, avanti, o sauro destrier, mio forte amico!*" "Forward, forward, O chestnut warhorse, my strong friend!" Not exactly the stuff to give the troops, huddled in mud and snow.

Every year there is a parade with floats, like the Macy's parade. Grazia's husband, beside working at Villa Selene as the cook and butler, used to manage the parade, a position of considerable importance. Oswaldo was a tall, handsome man, more like a Swede or Dane in appearance than an Italian. And one day, suddenly, he fell dead.

In the Summer there's open-air opera at Torre del Lago, where Puccini used to live, a short distance from Viareggio. There's a statue to Puccini and to the cigarette: he is smoking one in a holder. You may visit his house and see his music sheets, his bed, and photographs of his mistresses.

For fifteen years I have been coming to Viareggio and am thoroughly familiar with the beach, the restaurants, the shops and cafés . . . a place that "isn't even my type."

✤

Rosina the cleaning woman is highly temperamental, more like a Neapolitan than a Northerner. When anyone says anything she doesn't like, even Renato, she says "I'm going!" and starts taking off her apron.

This morning Vincenza gives us an account of Rosina's life, looking over her shoulder to be sure she doesn't hear. As a child Rosina was neglected. At fourteen she married a man who was "strange" . . . and a wife-beater. He struck her once so that she almost lost an eye. She had five miscarriages and gave birth twice, both girls. Five years ago her husband went off with another woman, leaving her with nothing but the clothes and two children to care for.

For five years Rosina has worked so hard and saved so well that she owns a dress shop and two houses: the house in which she lives and another that she has given to her older daughter. When not in the shop she works as a cleaning woman. Besides her daughters there are two aged relatives of whom she is the sole support.

After the day's work she goes dancing . . . every night and often till two in the morning. She dances the tango, as in the time of Rudolph Valentino. Vincenza illustrates by clenching an imaginary rose between her teeth.

We hear Rosina going downstairs, every step resounding through the house. She is a small woman but the floor shakes as she walks.

Vincenza says that Rosina is fifty. Once she asked her how she was able to dance after working all day. Rosina said, "I only need two or three hours of sleep."

She once remarked, "What a *romanzo* [novel] my life would make!" Vincenza comments that it is *buffo*, a comedy.

I tell Vincenza that my mother's life, also, would make a novel. She says that when Rosalind was still able to speak she would talk about her childhood in Russia, the rats that ran across the floor. I say yes, that has always been her obsession. Once at Villa Rosalinda I came into a room and found her telling my son Tony, who was only six or seven, about rats. She was saying that there were rats in the attic and if he went up there they would eat him. I put a stop to that storytelling. In the grip of her obsession all that concerned her was to express it, without thinking of the effect it might have on a child. Or perhaps she wanted him to share her fear.

Rosalind lies with her eyes closed as we talk. They say that "the unexamined life" is not worth living. She wasn't given to examining her life—instead she has had a life full of adventure.

Rosina looks in for a moment. Miriam speaks to her about our dog Veronica who died last summer when we were here in Italy. At the time Rosina expressed sympathy. So now Miriam is telling her that we buried Veronica in our yard with a gravestone.

Rosina says, "I have a cat, and the cat makes . . . " She puts out her tongue and moves it up and down, at the same time stroking her face. "But," she says, "I had a husband for thirty years and . . ." She hits her right arm with her left hand in a gesture that says, "Get going!", and kicks out with her right foot. "I had a husband but I don't remember him, so I'm not going to remember a cat."

Later, on our walk into town, Miriam and I take turns trying to imitate Rosina's kick. It isn't easy: the foot lifts, then goes out straight . . . a combination of pushing and kicking.

It's Sunday on the beach at Antaura and every place is taken. Each striped umbrella has people sitting or lying beneath; people of every age and shape. Many of the women, the younger ones, are wearing bikinis, the kind that have only a narrow strip covering the genitals and leaving the buttocks exposed.

The water is calm but cold. A tree has washed up on the sand and lies there like an octopus with its branches reaching out. A mile or two offshore there are sailboats and motorboats.

The Africans go by with their display cases of watches, combs, beads, and bracelets. The man with the fake Louis Vuitton bags. The man who sells ice cream: "Gelati graniti!" The one with coconut slices: "A lei coco!"

A black man stops by a woman with a child. "Compra," he says, "non é caro." "Buy. It isn't dear." She declines to buy. He asks her why. She repeats her refusal. He stands a while longer as if to compel her to change her mind, then moves away.

I'm reading *Whatever Became of . . . ?* by a man named Richard

Lamparski. I found it in a suitcase on the third floor among suit-cases and boxes brought here from San Alessio that were never unpacked. The book, with its biographies of people who were famous when she was young, must have been of engrossing inter-est to my mother.

> The beautiful prima donna of the Metropolitan Opera and motion pictures was born in 1904 in Deepwater, Missouri, an Ozark Mining town. She attended the Central High School in Kansas City and went on to Bush Conservatory of Music in Chicago from which she received a Doctorate of Music in 1923.

So begins the life of Gladys Swarthout. Rosalind also wanted to be a prima donna. How did she conceive the idea? Not in Russia . . . there women only cleaned and cooked—they weren't even allowed to go to school. It must have been after she came to America and was living in Brooklyn, taking the trolley every morning to the factory in Manhattan. While sewing tucks in shirts she dreamed of singing at the Metropolitan Opera.

> "The Orchid Lady of the Screen" was born in Texarkana, Texas, in 1896. She was educated at the Sacred Heart Academy in New Orleans where she was chosen Queen of the Mardi Gras. After her picture appeared on the cover of rotogravure sections of newspapers around the country she was signed to a contract with Vitagraph Pictures.

One day a man came to the factory where Rosalind was employed. He stood by the door as the women emerged, asking if any young lady would like to be in motion pictures.

She took a train to Fort Lee, New Jersey, where the studios were, and applied with other "hopefuls." She was listed as a "supernumerary," and she discovered that in order to be given parts you had to be able to dance, ride, and swim.

(I've told this story in other places but it is needed here, and why shouldn't a writer be allowed to tell the same story again from a different angle? Painters do it all the time: they paint the same woman, the same cathedral, the same water lilies, over and over again. The subject may be the same but the paintings are different . . . they're not the same thing.)

One day the leading actress was supposed to jump from a height into a tank of water and act as though she were drowning. She refused, and Rosalind took her place. She jumped and gave a striking performance, for she couldn't swim. After that she took swimming lessons, dance lessons, and riding lessons in Central Park. She attended an acting studio on 42nd Street.

Annette Kellerman and her troupe of bathing beauties were sailing for Jamaica to make a movie. When the "SS Almirante" pulled out of New York harbor Rosalind was aboard.

> The first woman to wear a one-piece bathing suit and to attempt to swim the English Channel was born in Australia in 1888.
>
> Crippled by polio shortly after birth, Annette had to wear large steel braces about three times the weight of those used today. She was, however, determined not to allow her affliction to break her health or her spirit.
>
> In 1914 she was starred by Universal Pictures in *Neptune's Daughter,* a great box office success . . .

Some years ago my mother tried to write an autobiography. "Jamaica," she exclaims, "what beauty for eyes that had never seen luscious tropical fruit and flowers!

"Every day we practiced swimming in the pool before work would begin. The practice session was witnessed by most of the young blades. Such a show of young beautiful girls in bathing suits was an unusual sight not to be missed—although we wore bathing stockings joining our costumes. It was only a discreet décolleté, still, for those Jamaican lads that constituted a risqué attire, and we were showered with sweet attention such as boxes of candy and occasional flowers. Amongst such sightseers was a prominent lawyer who asked a friend of the company to introduce him. He was most persistent and I finally met him.

"In the meantime our director was ready to make some of his scenes. He wanted to use the young members of the company as nude statues in harem scenes, avoiding costly marble or gypsum statuary. Some accepted and a few refused, since we were supposed to act as mermaids only—I for one could not imagine myself in such a role. I felt that my life would be irrevocably ruined, and I flatly refused. My job terminated with that refusal. I broke my contract according to the indiscernible second page that hardly anyone reads—anyway not a seventeen-year-old girl."

So she sailed back to a flat in New York. The "prominent lawyer" wrote to her: "Heavy six-page letters would arrive almost twice weekly. We lived at that time in a garden apartment on East Broadway. The letter would fall with a thud and I would eagerly pick it up and go into my room and read his outpouring of endearments to me who never had any experience and never enough love at home. Mother certainly had no time for such nonsense— it was too hard a life, caring for her large family."

All her life Rosalind would be waiting for the love she never had at home.

> It eluded us then, but that's no matter—tomorrow we will run faster, stretch out our arms farther . . . and one fine morning—

Vincenza speaks in a loud voice close to her ear: "Are you tired? Do you wish to go to bed?" She nods slightly, and Vincenza calls to Grazia, and they lift her between them and carry her from the chair to the bed.

2

We have decided not to have a car while we're in Italy. A rented car sitting in the drive at so many thousand lire a day demands to be used, and we may not want to go anywhere. Besides, you don't see the scenery when you're driving, you have to pay attention to the road.

So we took the bus to Pisa. Miriam wanted to visit the Musèo dell 'Opera, but it was closed when we got there, so we had lunch, then visited the Campo Santo. We never tire of looking at "The

Triumph of Death," the Last Judgment, Hell, and the anchorites living among caves and rocks. Scholars say that Chaucer visited Pisa when "The Triumph of Death" was being painted. When he came to write the tales of the pilgrims he must have recalled these men and women riding toward three corpses in progressive stages of decay.

The Musèo opened at three. There was a "Madonna del Colloquio" by Giovanni Pisano, remarkable, said the printed guide, for the position of the child on the arm of the Madonna and the "speaking looks" that gave the sculpture its name. In another room there was an ivory Madonna and child by the same artist with an original "solution": the sculpture follows the curve of the elephant's tusk, the Madonna leaning back to balance the child she is holding in her arms. The pose is natural and charming, but I am thinking of the elephant. The human race in 1300 didn't think twice about killing an elephant for its tusks. Our thinking hasn't advanced much since that time, and the elephant is about to disappear. How does the Madonna feel about the extinction of the elephant? Does her son have anything to say about animals? I don't recall that he does.

Vincenza says that Rosalind had a good night. She slept and this morning she ate her broth. But then there was a crisis: she couldn't breathe because of the liquid in her chest and her lips were blue. Vincenza gave her a pill to slow the heart beat, another to lower the blood pressure, and a third for her stomach. The crisis passed.

Renato comes into the bedroom with a new medicine. He has also brought a bunch of red, long-stemmed roses for Rosalind. He goes out of the room and there's an explosion of voices ﹒ ﹒ ﹒ the voice of Rosina raised in expostulation: "Calm yourself! I am not in forced labor." Apparently he asked her to bring a vase for the roses and she's not doing it fast enough.

Vincenza leans over Rosalind, persuading her to put out her

tongue. She gives her a capsule for the catarrh and holds a glass of water to her mouth. Rosalind swallows with gurgling sounds.

Vincenza takes Rosalind's pulse, looking at her watch. She moves Rosalind's head to an upright position on the pillow—it keeps tilting to one side.

There's another outbreak in the hall. Rosina, who beside cleaning the house also does the laundry, wants Renato to wear his cotton underwear, but he insists on wearing woolen underwear, for he is always cold. The house is still being heated . . . at the end of June!

Vincenza goes out of the room to take part in the discussion.

The radio is playing a piano concerto. Mozart is good, but the comedy of Renato and Rosina is also good.

This morning I called my brother in Canada and gave him an account of Mother's condition. He was grateful—he hadn't been able to get past the old woman downstairs, Grazia's mother-in-law who acts as switchboard operator. It was the Engineer's idea when he lived here to rig up a switchboard so that incoming calls could be monitored, as in an office. So the first thing a caller hears is the old woman croaking.

I asked my brother how he was. He said, fine. He has changed his doctor and everyone is astonished at his recovery.

I gave him a message from Renato: he mustn't do exercises.

Herbert believes in exercise. A room of his apartment in Toronto has been fitted out as a gym. The walls are lined with pictures of himself as a young man wearing trunks, in body-building poses.

Renato has asked me to call the hospital in Toronto where Herbert was treated after his heart attack. I am to get in touch with the doctor and tell him to tell Herbert not to do exercises. I listened to this idea with amazement. I told Renato that I couldn't undertake to do this . . . it was impossible. But I would pass on his message to Herbert.

✤

In the afternoon we go to the beach. Sandra Gattai, the daughter of Attilia, Renato's niece, is there with her six-year-old daughter, Cristina, who's big for her age and very shy. She doesn't answer when we speak to her.

Sandra's husband, Cèsare, is an engineer. Sandra teaches English in a *licèo*. A few years ago they went to Venezuela where Cèsare worked on a building project, but the company went out of business and Sandra and Cèsare lost everything. They returned to this part of the world. Cèsare took a job teaching science in a school in Lucca while Sandra taught English in Barga. This is in the mountains, a hard drive in winter.

Now Sandra has found a teaching position in Viareggio, and they have bought another, bigger house in a more pleasant neighborhood. And Cèsare has found another engineering job. But it is in Naples. He has to be in Naples most of the week and is home only on weekends.

Renato's friend Emilio Berti, l'Avvocato (the Lawyer), found a position for Cèsare in Viareggio as superintendent of bus lines, an important position that would have paid well, but Cèsare didn't want it . . . he wanted a position in his field, engineering.

So Sandra and Cèsare will be spending most of the time away from each other. This can happen to young married people these days when women as well as men hold jobs. Living is expensive, and a couple with a child can use the double income.

The Woman from Wittenberg

There are many Germans traveling in Italy. The night before last Miriam and I had dinner at La Casina, the restaurant in the park we go to for a change from Montecatini. As we were having coffee a woman at the next table walked over and spoke to us. We think she must have heard our conversation and that we were discussing Germans. If so, she could have heard nothing to please her, for when the subject comes up Miriam says that they haven't changed, they are the same racists they were in the time of Hitler. I say that I don't think so, the young ones are different. But I say this without conviction.

The woman who appeared at our table and stood there saying something was about fifty, blonde, with a thin face and glasses. She excused herself, she didn't want to disturb us, she was sorry . . . but she was German.

I didn't know what to make of this, but I assured her that we weren't prejudiced, and invited her to sit down and have a coffee.

She accepted gladly and proceeded to give an account of herself. She was in Viareggio to study the Italian language. Her husband didn't pay her much attention . . . he was an important man and very busy, so she felt that she ought to have an interest of her own. She wanted to be an interpreter, though she had a degree in economics. Her husband's field was robotics . . . the use of robots in the factory or home. His work had taken them to San Diego in California.

She told us again that her husband didn't pay her much attention. They lived in Wittenberg and had two children, sons, who were now grown men. They were studying different subjects. One was an engineer . . . I don't recall what she said the other was. Children were a big problem today in Germany. The law said that you had to support them in whatever line of study they chose to follow, and if they changed their mind at thirty and wanted to take up something else you had to keep on supporting them. One of her sons was interrupting his studies in order to go to New Zealand. Two years ago he had gone to Australia, and now he wanted to see New Zealand and they would have to pay his expenses.

This description of German law sounded improbable, but we agreed that living with children these days could be difficult.

The trouble she said, was over-population.

I was trying to follow her. I said that in the United States we weren't able to keep up with the population . . . a large number of young people were not being educated.

She asked if we'd been to the South of France lately. The South was black. The only solution was to sterilize those people.

I sensed that Miriam's temperature was rising and she was about to explode. She did speak, but calmly, explaining to the German woman that no one had a right to sterilize people. She listened as though this were an original, unheard-of point of view. "You are very intelligent," she told Miriam.

We parted from her outside the restaurant and walked back to the villa. It was a while before either of us spoke. Then Miriam said, "It seems that they never learn."

The next morning at breakfast we told Grazia about our meeting with the German woman. She said, "We Italians don't like the Germans." Then she told the following story.

When she was a girl of thirteen the Germans declared Viareggio a "black zone," that is, a zone you were forbidden to enter. It was one of the places where the Allies might make a landing. Grazia and other people from Viareggio went into the hills, to the village of Santa Anna di Stazema.

One day her sister came to the village, having walked all the way from the place where she was staying, to tell them that the Germans were coming to Santa Anna di Stazema and they should leave at once. The partisans had killed two German soldiers and the Germans were planning to retaliate. Very few believed the rumor, but Grazia did and went away with her sister.

The next day the Germans came to Santa Anna di Stazema. They rounded up all the people, men, women, and children, and gathered them in the square in front of the church. Then they machine-gunned them. Some pleaded with the soldiers saying, "I am a mother. You have a mother of your own." But the German would kill the mother in front of her child. They made a fire with gasoline and threw children, alive, onto the flames.

One child, when the shooting started, fell under the bodies of her mother and father and her brothers and sisters. She was covered with blood. The Germans came looking for those who were still alive, to finish them off, but the child lay as one dead and they passed by. It was remarkably clever of the child: she was the only one to survive the massacre of Santa Anna di Stazema.

More than three hundred people were killed. Today if you go to Santa Anna di Stazema there is a monument in the square in front of the church, and photographs of those who were killed.

"The war is over," Grazia says, "and now there is tourism in Italy. The Germans come to Viareggio. The young men go to bed with the young women . . . that's to be expected. And we Italians are polite and wait on them. But we do not like them. There are many among us who remember. How can you ever forget such things?"

The sun is blazing from a light blue sky. People are standing in the water . . . few actually swim.

Three young women in bikinis walk along the beach and the men look them over. There are always three, I tell Miriam. She questions this and points out two together and one who is walking by herself. Yes, I say, but you'll see there are often three. As in war novels . . . *Three Comrades* . . . or stories about schooldays.

Italians are good-looking. Even the old ones who are thin or fat and bent out of shape seem to remember when they were good-looking. They care how others see them and try to make the best of what's left. Not like Americans who walk about in a cloak of invisibility . . . as doctors, accountants, truck drivers. Italians know they are being looked at; you can't go through life trying not to be seen; you are here definitely, a part of the universe, so you should try to make as pleasing an impression as you can. You owe it to the others.

When I first lived among Italians I thought their regard for "la bella figura" symptomatic of lightness of intellect. Now I think it means that life is real . . . eternity is here and now. At any rate, the physicality of the Italians strikes me as a lot more desirable than the abstraction of other races whose devotion to an ideal spoils all the pleasure in life and turns out, after all, to be symptomatic of pride, greed, rage, or some other vice. There are people living in

Missoula who think that because they owe money to the bank and the car won't start they are morally superior. This could be a mistake.

A man with a brown skin and wrinkled face, apparently an Algerian, goes by carrying dresses on hangers. Some of the beach peddlers wear picturesque costumes and hats. A black man wearing a gown and a straw hat sits in the shade of an umbrella, bows his head, and rests.

✿

On returning to the villa we find Renato stationed outside Rosalind's room. She has influenza and a temperature of 37.4 Centigrade. The doctor was here . . . she was calling for him. Vincenza also came—she left at three but came back for the emergency.

There are sounds from the room . . . sounds of pain: "Oh, oh!" We go in. Rosalind is lying on her back, looking up. I say a few words to her and her eyes look into mine as though she wants me to do something to ease the pain, but I'm not the one she needs, there's nothing I can do.

Vincenza says that it appears to be the left arm. Rosalind's hands are swollen and the pain can be atrocious. She puts some ointment on the arm . . . it has withered . . . loose flesh over the bone . . . and massages it. But Rosalind continues to cry "Oh, oh!" Vincenza lifts Rosalind's right hand and places it on different parts of her body. "Is the pain here? Here?" Finally Rosalind utters a sound that Vincenza interprets to mean "Behind." She is suffering from the ulcers in the lower part of her back.

Usually when she is suffering this way they move her to the chair, but to move her with a fever could be dangerous. Vincenza begins to work on her lower body and I leave the room. Miriam stays for a few minutes. Afterwards she tells me that the lower part of Rosalind's body is swollen, her stomach and the whole leg from the hip down. She has "edema," fluid collected from bad circulation, but this, Miriam says, appears more normal than the upper body which has withered away so that there is only skin and bone.

My mother's temperature is down and she is sitting up in the chair. We ask Grazia if there have been other such crises. She says yes, several. Six weeks ago Rosalind's heart appeared to have stopped—there was no pulse. For five minutes. They threw the windows open to let in air. The male nurse happened to be in attendance. He gave her an injection and the vital signs returned. A miracle!

Miriam says that yesterday when Rosalind had a temperature she thought she heard her say, "I am dead." Is it possible that she remembers something of the time, six weeks ago, when she was between life and death? That they are confused in her mind?

We go in to see her. She is sitting in the chair, propped with pillows, sleeping. I make a drawing. As I outline her features it becomes a drawing of a stranger. The face is longer and narrower than the face of the woman I remember. No one could tell from looking at her in what country or century she was born. The hair is white and thinned out, the scalp showing. The eyes closed, the head tilted forward, the mouth slightly open and twisted down in the right corner. Her cheeks have been rouged. This is grotesque but, who knows, she may want it so.

The drawing is of a stage of human life, extreme old age in fifth-century Greece, medieval France, nineteenth-century Russia. The human being simplified . . . the wrinkles ironed out. The skin stretched over the bone is as smooth as a child's.

> —Avez-vous observé que maints cercueils de vieilles
> Sont presque aussi petits que celui d'un enfant?

❖

Last night the United States lost to Austria, 2-0. Whatever the Americans had learned about soccer in their previous matches they seemed to have forgotten in the second half. They kicked the ball down the field . . . to nobody, and therefore to the Austrians. When the goalie had the ball he took time to see that all the players were in their places. He should have got the ball out immediately to the players, who should have been running. When the Americans came near the Austrian goal they didn't know how to attack . . . their forwards couldn't shoot.

If the U.S. are going to play international football they need to use some of the South Americans who are wandering footloose in New York and Los Angeles, to show them how. They need to play frequently against teams such as the Austrians so they can learn their tricks. The Austrians, for example, are expert at fouling. When they aren't tripping you they know how to fall and double up, giving the impression of being *in extremis*.

The Americans need to learn that in international competition the object is not to play the game but to win.

The Italians also played tonight, winning their match against Czechoslovakia, 2-0. Cars came racing both ways on Viale Carducci, blowing horns and waving flags. There were some motorcyclists too, taking their lives in their hands.

We watched with Grazia from the top of the stairs in front of the villa. She spoke of the time that Italy won the World Cup. Renato's brother Giorgio, who used to play center forward for Milan, became so excited over the victory that he jumped in the air and fell and broke a leg.

Giorgio was living here at the time. He had lights strung along the sidewalk in front of the villa and a banner hung from the top floor: "Glory to the Blues of Milan!"

As we watch the cars racing by there is a scream as though someone has been hit. Or like the scream of an animal. Grazia and I run outside. There is no one lying by the road. There is, however, a woman dressed in white and carrying a large handbag. In the evening on our way home Miriam and I have seen one woman or another on the sidewalk near the villa. A car draws up and a conversation takes place.

Grazia speaks to her: "Have you seen a cat that was hit by a car?" She shakes her head, no.

What strikes me afterwards is the matter-of-factness with which Grazia spoke to the woman. As though she had a right to be there, like anyone else.

Reading Gill's life of Wordsworth . . . The book is in mint condition—I was the first to take it out of the library though it had been there for two years.

When it returns and the others ask where it's been, what a tale it will have to tell! "I've been to Italy, going to the beach every day and eating at Lidino." How envious they'll be, those wretched books smelling of hamburger and onions, with their marks of dirty fingers and the thoughts of students scribbled in the margins.

Wordsworth accepted a government job as Distributor of Stamps. From then on he sucked up to the rich and powerful. And this was the poet who in his youth hailed the French Revolution! "Just for a handful of silver he left us."

Gill says that's just the point . . . it was only a handful of silver. We shouldn't be hard on Wordsworth . . . the job didn't pay well.

❧

Today the sea is rough and the red flags are up. The lifeguard explains, "C'è una buca." "There's a hole." The waves dig out the sea floor and someone who's a poor swimmer can suddenly find himself out of his depth. Moreover, there's a current that pulls you out to sea. It is "molto pericoloso," very dangerous.

I've written elsewhere about the time my son Tony was caught in the current and I would have been unable to save him. The lifeguards came out and took him to shore. I think about it every time I swim at Antaura. I know what Laocoon felt as he struggled with the serpents that were coiled around him and his sons.

Yesterday a young man drowned at Viareggio. He leaves a young wife who is pregnant. Vincenza says that he ate a pizza and went swimming soon afterwards. She says that you must wait for three hours after eating before you go swimming. Vincenza is a good nurse but she isn't a swimmer.

I ask the lifeguard where the current is . . . a hundred meters out? No, another lifeguard says, much less. Fifty? Yes. On calm days is there a current? No.

I explain that I'm a writer and that is why I am asking questions. The lifeguards nod understandingly. Italians like to know the reasons for what you do. Keeping your reasons to yourself is unfriendly . . . to ask questions and not explain would be rude. Now that they know that I'm a writer they're pleased to have been asked about the "buca" and the current.

I'm through with the Wordsworth, and Miriam has finished *The Private Papers of Henry Ryecroft* and passed it on.

> Never again shall I shake hands with man or woman who is not in truth my friend.

Ryecroft has broken with "society," which he never saw much of in any case. He won't pretend to be glad to see people with whom he has nothing in common and whom he secretly despises. This appeals to me: with two or three exceptions, I have very little to do with people at the place where I work—they certainly aren't friends. I say hello when one of them comes down the corridor and there's no way to avoid meeting. That is all. And Miriam and I don't have much to do with our neighbors. We agree with Henry Ryecroft that in the absence of friends you shouldn't make do with second-best. I think it is Wordsworth who speaks of "greetings where no kindness is." Going through the motions of friendship with those who aren't your friend takes the joy out of life. It's like living with someone you don't love. And besides, it prevents you meeting someone you might.

Rosalind is making sounds of pain . . . a sound between "Oh" and "Ah." Vincenza locates the pain as being in her head and gives her an aspirin, using the pill-crusher that I contributed to the cause. At least I was able to contribute something!

Rosalind's mouth moves and gurgling sounds come out. She coughs and seems to be choking. There's an anxious look in her eyes. They express infinite but not patient suffering.

She is choking. Vincenza says "Calma, calma," lifting Rosalind's head from the pillow. She is gasping for breath.

❖

There are people and incidents of no importance, "string too short to be saved" as Donald Hall once wrote.

Yesterday Vincenza locked herself out of her house and had to climb in through a window. She didn't have time to have lunch between her job here and her job at the hospital. What a day!

During the night a thief drained the gas from the tank of the old Mercedes Renato leaves parked in the lane behind the villa.

This morning Rosina is in good voice, singing "Come back to Sorrento" as she clumps up and down stairs with her mop and bucket. She alternates with whistling.

There are the people and incidents you see in the street. The old man wheeling a bicycle with a small boy sitting in the basket on the handlebars . . . The boy was singing happily as the old man, obviously his grandfather, wheeled him along. And now as we sit in the café having a Campari and soda we see them again, crossing the street, the old man wheeling the bicycle with the boy on the handlebars, coming up from the beach. They are like characters in an Italian movie.

There's the stout middle-aged lady who rides her bicycle on the esplanade every afternoon at five. In front of her, and around her, scampers a black Cocker Spaniel. He goes running in every direction, barking, investigating, meeting other dogs, and returns to catch up with his mistress as she pedals sedately, as happy as a dog can be.

❖

English cookery is the wholesomest and the most appetizing known to any temperate clime.

When I was a boy in colonial Jamaica we were told that everything English was superior. How vastly the world has changed, and in such a short time! Henry Ryecroft thinks that nothing can equal the English form of government, English home life and, of all things, English "Puritanism." He praises the "delicacy" of English women. This is ironic when you recall that the author of the book, George Gissing, married a prostitute.

Little girls should be taught cooking and baking more assiduously than they are taught to read.

That does it! Into the dust-bin with Henry.

Miriam and I discuss with Vincenza yesterday's high school exam, the dreaded Maturità. Her daughter took the mathematics exam. It was extremely difficult: only four or five students out of 112 think they passed. The students came out of the examination crying and vomiting. Angela, who stays with Rosalind at night, also has a daughter who took the exam. It was a disaster.

Vincenza explains that much depends on the makeup of the commission that sets the exams. This year the commission is bad . . . drawn from everywhere, people who have no knowledge of the local schools and their methods. The students work with a certain teacher for five years, then the exam is set by someone who has a different method and expectations.

You have to pass the Maturità with good grades in all subjects to be admitted to a university. There is only the state university—there are no private universities, the students have protested against there being any. They say it would be unjust: people with money would be able to send their children to a university and others would be excluded. So there are no universities except those administered by the state, and entrance to these is determined by merit only, that is, by exams.

So students themselves are maintaining the system that sends them out of the room crying and vomiting. The state system prevents many from entering a university who have done well in one subject but are failing another. A tremendous waste of human resources . . . all in the name of justice.

❧

Today was our fifth wedding anniversary. This evening we walked the length of Viale Carducci looking at the Saturday night crowd, young ones, old ones, on foot and on bicycle. We agreed once more that Italians are good to look at . . . because they are living with enjoyment, that's what it is.

We have dinner at Lidino, which is open on Saturday but closed on weekday nights. Miriam orders spaghetti with white clam sauce. I have fish soup. Then we share a *frito misto*, the specialty of the house, a dish of fried shrimps, mussels, crayfish, squid, and small fishes. A lettuce and tomato salad on the side. For dessert, balls of vanilla ice cream with a coffee ice cream center. Then a cappuccino for her and espresso for me.

I tell Suzanna that it's our wedding anniversary and she brings us glasses of champagne, compliments of the house.

I am sitting across from Miriam. Behind her the sea, which has been breaking roughly all day, is somber and gray with a white surf. The sun is going down quickly, a red ball on the horizon. Suddenly it drops.

❧

> He felt that his torture was caused by his being pushed into that black hole, but even more by his being unable to crawl into it himself.
>
> Leo Tolstoy, *The Death of Ivan Ilyich*

Looking on as Vincenza gives Rosalind her medicine and she chokes trying to swallow, listening to her cries of pain and her attempts to form a word, "Help!", looking into her eyes, I am aware how frightened she is of dying, how, in spite of being racked by pain, in her arms and legs, in her stomach and back, she clings to life, to her suffering, in terror of the black hole into which she is being pushed.

He was prevented from crawling into it by the belief that his life had been a good one. This defense of the life he had lived was the hindrance that kept him from moving ahead, and it caused him more torture than anything else.

Why is she so afraid of dying? Because, like Ivan Ilyich, she cannot imagine a better life than the one she has had. This is why she cannot give it up and continues to suffer.

3

We spent the morning trying to get through to Alitalia to confirm our reservations. Impossible . . . the lines were "occupato." Renato was in his study with the Avvocato. I told him the trouble we were having; he called his travel agent, and the agent called back in a few minutes to say that our reservations had been confirmed. Renato said, "Tell me when there's something to be done. Don't try to do it yourself, you don't know how."

We spent the afternoon on the beach. At 5 o'clock Sandra Gattai, her daughter Cristina, and Sandra's mother Attilia, came to take us to see Sandra's new house. She and Cèsare moved in only a month ago. The house is impressive, solidly built—the previous owner meant to live there for a long time and took pains. Sandra is happy, too, about her new neighbors: in the last house she and Cèsare quarreled with the people who lived above them. The new house has three floors with no one living above, a two-car garage, and a paved area in the back they call the garden with a tree growing in the middle.

We sat in this area and discussed Rosalind and Renato, how he's trying to prolong her life. If he hears of a new medicine he must get it at once. What's he going to do when she's gone? What will he have to live for?

I tell the story of Rosalind's coming to America at the age of fourteen, bringing her two younger sisters with her. How she worked in the garment district, then became an actress, that is, an extra in motion pictures. She climbs the ladder to a platform on which bushes have been placed and a canvas painted to look like a cliff. Looking down at the water and the faces staring up at her . . . It's a long way down, and what if she misses?

The director shouts through the megaphone. She takes a breath and steps off. Everything flashes by. She comes to the surface choking and flailing. A wonderful bit of acting . . . Then they realize that she's drowning and pull her out.

Sandra drove us to see the Borbone estate in the middle of Viareggio that used to belong to the royal family of Austria and now belongs to the Barsantis. All but the Villa Borbone . . . that was donated by the Engineer, Benvenuto, to the Commune to be used for cultural purposes. But the remaining property, a hundred hectares and the buildings on them, is to be divided among the heirs. Renato's younger brother Giorgio, who played football in Milan, is to have the bulk of the property. The rest is to be divided among Renato; Renato's niece Attilia; another niece, Stefanella, who lives in Rome; and a fifth party whom Sandra refers to as "a stranger."

Nothing can be done, none of them can inherit anything, until Giorgio, who inherited forty-eight per cent of the property, sits down with the others and they agree who is to have what parcel of land and which buildings. There is more than enough to go around, but Giorgio refuses to meet with the others. He doesn't answer letters. Sandra sticks messages on his front door asking him to meet her, but he doesn't answer. She once made an appointment with Giorgio and his lawyer to meet on a Sunday, but he failed to show up. Meanwhile some peasants are living in the buildings free of charge, and the lawyers are dragging out the business.

Renato as the oldest surviving brother stood next in line to inherit, but the Engineer willed him a sum to be paid every month by the construction company and to cease with death. The Engineer never married, and he disapproved of marriage for your estate went to your wife's relatives. So he passed over Renato and left the bulk of the estate to Giorgio who isn't married and everyone says is "pazzo," crazy.

Renato sometimes says ruefully that he lost a fortune when he married Rosalind, and it happens to be true. The Borbone property isn't all that Giorgio inherited. There is the company in Venezuela. He inherited the company offices in Rome, a shipyard in Viareggio, and a share in the beach property, Antura, Principe, and so on. He owns an orange grove in Florida. Moreover, the Engineer left the Villa Selene to be divided among the family, so that no one really owns it. Giorgio has a part of that too.

Sandra let us off at Montecatini. We had dinner and walked back on Viale Carducci. The sidewalk was crowded and Miriam said, "The air is throbbing." And it seemed to be, as though the crowd had a single life that could be felt and heard. But in a few minutes we arrived at a circle of onlookers and a band of musicians. They were dark-skinned; they wore dark felt hats, serapes, and espadrilles. Some wore their hair long down their back. One was playing a guitar, another an instrument with ten strings like a mandolin, another a ukulele. The drummer beat the drum with one hand; in the other he held a wooden flute of reeds tied together on which he blew emphatically, making a shrill sound.

They were "Peruvianos." One of them who wasn't wearing a serape, apparently the manager, went around the circle with an open instrument case into which people were throwing thousand-lire notes. They liked the music.

Downtown with Renato driving the old Mercedes . . . Hair-raising, for his vision is poor and he drifts across the median line into the path of oncoming traffic.

We went with him to the travel agency where he asked for Vittorio. A young man appeared, smiling, and gave us a slip of paper, a note to the airline saying that our reservations were confirmed and that they should be upgraded if possible, for I was an important person . . . "Premio Pulitzer Prize."

Miriam and I could hardly keep a straight face. Renato always introduces me as "Premio Pulitzer Prize." At first I thought he was joking, then I realized he was serious. And the people to whom he introduced me took it seriously. I didn't try to tell them why they shouldn't. I let them think a Pulitzer Prize was important, since thinking so made them happy.

We parted from Renato—we were to meet again at Tito's for lunch. Then we walked to the post office to mail some books to the U. S. The clerk had white hair and looked at us over his spectacles like a clerk in a novel by Dickens. In sealing the book-mailing envelopes Miriam had covered some printed words. These had to be uncovered, which he did carefully with a fingernail. He looked up the reduced tariff for books, weighed one of the packages, wrote down the postage . . . on the wrong package . . . corrected his error, and tied the package with string. Meanwhile a line had formed behind us. I'll say this for them, they were patient. You have to be when you go to the post office in Italy.

We went looking for oil and vinegar cruets but couldn't find the store where we'd seen them. The heat was intense. We were looking for a place to sit when we saw Renato across the street, ensconced outside a café. We went over and sat with him. Everyone who came by seemed to know him. A woman stood by the table and talked to him, leaning over and patting his cheek from time to time to emphasize a point.

He was reading *La Nazione Viareggio*. What was this? A photograph of the Villa Rosalinda where he and Rosalind had lived for eighteen years . . . with an advertisement:

Clinica Gastronomica

la

Dispensa

organizza:

Matrimoni, Cerimonie, Meeting Aziendali

The villa had been turned into a banquet hall. For business meetings and weddings . . . "con Cappella Privata," with a private chapel. He kept staring at the ad.

Rosalind shouldn't see this. No, we said, she shouldn't. We didn't say that she wouldn't be able to read it or even see the picture.

The Avvocato joined us at Tito's for lunch. We were early and had the restaurant to ourselves. Miriam ordered a cold fish salad she remembered from her last visit to Tito's. Renato and the Avvocato ordered steaks, big ones, real "Fiorentinos," for the Avvocato has been ordered by his doctor to eat steak to reduce his weight. He is suffering from a slipped disk . . . at least, that's the diagnosis. "I'd rather have spaghetti," he said, looking at the dish I'd ordered. Following this I had fish broiled and served on a skewer. Miriam had a steak too, but much smaller than the large portions Renato and the Avvocato were devouring as though they wouldn't be allowed to eat like that at home.

According to the Avvocato, the high school exam about which there had been so much discussion because it was so difficult was three times as difficult when he was young.

Renato went to the men's room and the Avvocato said, "Renato is a great man. There are all sorts of people in Viareggio. Sometimes you'll see someone who's bent under his woes, with a doleful expression. He sees Renato and all at once he smiles."

I could testify to the truth of this. I had recently paid a visit to a man I had known for thirty years and thought of as a friend. I found that he had changed—perhaps it would be truer to say that certain tendencies in his character had become stronger. A change in quantity can be a change in kind and he was no longer the man I knew: he was self-centered, cold, repellent.

I was thinking about this and musing on the transitory nature of friendship and of life in general. "You look sad," Renato remarked. I hadn't been conscious of feeling sad. After all, the sun was shining on the hills above Viareggio. I had just come from swimming, and I was with the woman I loved.

But still there was the vibration of a thought like an instrument in an orchestra playing off key. A friendship was over and I would probably never see that man again. I felt that life had been diminished. It was this vibration Renato felt and extracted from the rest. To this he turned his attention, and he drew my attention to it, revealing my sadness to me so that instead of going through the day vaguely troubled I was able to put my finger on the cause, isolate a thought and separate it from the mass.

It wasn't life that was making me sad . . . not even my mother's life coming to an end, for there was nothing sad about it. Her life had been a *romanzo*, a story that was ending as such stories must.

No, it wasn't life . . . there was nothing wrong with life. The trouble was people, and there wasn't much you could do about them. But you could do something about yourself: you could take care not to become that kind of person . . . the friend who was no longer a friend, absorbed in his thoughts and with no affection for others. Life didn't have to be that way . . . you could live according to reason.

When Renato pointed out that I looked sad he restored the rule of reason, which is never sad, and I became one of the people who, upon seeing Renato, smiled.

We did not tell her we were leaving—Renato asked us not to, it would upset her greatly. As it turned out we could not have said goodbye in any case, for she had two injections the night before, one for the pain in her leg and one to make her sleep, and today she was still sleeping.

Going Back

I

> Breathes there the man, with soul so dead,
> Who never to himself hath said,
> This is my own, my native land!
>
> Walter Scott

Y es, Walter, there breathes, for surely America has been kinder to me than my native land.

> And what is our nation?
> The place where we were born
> or the one that permits us to live?

When our father died and the will was read my brother and I had been disinherited. He had left us a few hundred pounds—the rest of his large estate went to our stepmother. She had arranged matters so, and the day after the funeral she sent us packing.

No one seemed to care what would become of us. A year later, when the opportunity presented itself, I left Jamaica and did not look back.

But I would dream I was back. If you drove east from Kingston, leaving the harbor behind, and went through a tunnel, the open sea lay before you with long waves rolling in. I was walking on the sand, picking up seashells and cramming them in my pockets. There was a flat brown seed with a black rim called a horse-eye, and yellow seeds that were like polished stone. There were shells of many shapes and colors lying in the sand. But a voice called to me . . . it was time to come away.

I was at the house of my Jamaican relatives, the Fletchers, where my brother and I stayed for a while. I was on the veranda and people were sitting nearby. I told them that a real estate agent had telephoned to find out if the apartment my mother kept in New York were for sale. I spoke angrily about people who made a living from death. My mother smiled . . . she was a passionate speaker herself. She was sitting apart from the others, looking young and slender, in a dress of the kind they wore in the thirties. I was happy to see her . . . it wasn't everyone whose mother looked so beautiful and young.

Shortly after this, my cousin Douglas telephoned from Jamaica. There were people at the university in Kingston who would like to hear me give a lecture and a reading of my poems. He knew that my brother and I had been treated cruelly, but . . . I assured him that I no longer had any ill feelings. All that had happened long ago.

❧

Kingston is crowded and dangerous. But even in the suburbs where well-to-do people such as the Fletchers live, no one is safe. Doors and windows are barred. At night the householders lock themselves in their bedrooms so if robbers break in they will take what they want and leave without harming anyone. Crime and violence are symptomatic of the extreme poverty of the island.

In the eighteenth century the British considered Jamaica a more valuable possession than all their American colonies: the island produced cane sugar. Today the sugar you have with your coffee at a hotel comes in paper packets from Miami. When Miriam and I were traveling with the Fletchers, one morning at breakfast

Hazel complained about this. Jamaica was a sugar-producing country . . . why import it? Douglas said that the people who owned the hotel had forty other hotels all over the world. They got the sugar for a penny a packet—it would cost Jamaicans five pennies to make it. There was nothing he or anyone else could do about it.

While the economy has declined the population has been increasing. Today there are more than two million people living on an island a hundred and forty-six miles long from east to west and fifty-one miles across at the widest. Nothing, it seems, can be done to slow the growth of population. A woman has to "have out her number" the people say, otherwise she will be sick.

The main industry is tourism, and when there are hurricanes or the tide of violence rises this source of income dwindles to a trickle. Foreigners come to Jamaica for a vacation and stay at one of the hotels at Negril, Montego Bay, or Ocho Rios. They swim, go horseback riding, or play golf, and go home to talk of the fine time they had. They don't go to Kingston. There you may see thousands who are unemployed standing about in the streets. The buildings are run down, areas that used to be residential have turned into slums. The countryside is no better: the country people barely scratch out a living.

Douglas and Hazel are informed about everything and seem to know everyone. Douglas is a lawyer, of so many kinds that it made my head spin to hear: conveyancing, that is, real estate . . . probate and administration; corporate and international law; banking and insurance. He has taken an active part in government. In colonial days he was a member of the Legislative Council. After Independence he served as a senator and minister in the Jamaican government. From 1972 to '75 he was Jamaican Ambassador to the United States. Three years of being diplomatic in Washington were enough—Hazel longed to be home with her garden.

The Fletchers have five children. The oldest, Peter, is a surgeon at the university in Kingston. Their other son, Richard, is an economist and lives in Washington, D.C. Their daughter Andrea, a computer programmer, lives in Miami. Suzanne is a doctor and practices in Nashville, Tennessee. And Christine is a systems engineer: she lives in Kingston and works with computers. All these children, except Andrea, are married and have children of their own. Douglas and Hazel are like the good people one reads about in the Bible whose tribe is still increasing. And all this came of his sitting at a table every evening when he was a boy, doing algebra and studying Latin, and her cultivating her garden.

Douglas's mother was my father's sister Edith, and when Douglas was a young man he was articled to my father. That was how you became a solicitor, as lawyers were called: you apprenticed yourself to a solicitor and took examinations. My father, Aston Simpson, was one of the best known lawyers on the island. He and H.A.L. Lake were famous for their encounters. When word went around that Simpson and Lake were appearing against each other, people dropped what they were doing and went to hear.

My father's brother Bertie was also a lawyer, but he would shuffle some papers and be off to his other job as mayor of Kingston which he found more rewarding. His way of arguing a case was to pound on a table and shout. Douglas decided that he could never be the "court lawyer" my father was, nor pound and shout like Bertie. A judge once told him that he could tell from his face whether or not he thought his client innocent. So he gave up going to court and took up conveyancing, et cetera, instead.

Hazel comes over where Miriam and I are sitting: she has some photographs to show us. The first is of my father, his parents, and three of his sisters. My father's father has spectacles and a mustache. He appears to be white, but a bit dusky—Jamaicans are a mixture of races. He is standing and looking warily at the camera as though life has been a little too much for him, but perhaps it is only the cares of a family. His hand is resting on the shoulder of his wife, who is seated. There can be no doubt about her antecedents: she is, as the dictionary puts it, "a person of mixed Caucasian and Negro ancestry." A handsome woman . . . her face reveals nothing of what she is thinking. Three of her daughters are around her. One, Ethel, is missing. But present are Edith, who would be Douglas's mother, and Inis, who would surprise everyone by becoming a nurse—in the age of Victoria unmarried women from good families did not go to work, they lived with their relatives. It made for a pursed look about the mouth, expressions of disapproval, and rushing off to one's room to cry. The third sister is May who also did not marry and would come and take care of my brother and me when our mother was away.

The older son, Bertie, isn't in the picture, but Aston is. My father, a boy of ten or thereabouts, is standing to the right of his father and leaning against a pedestal with his legs crossed. The pose is supposed to be nonchalant: he stares straight at the camera, unlike his father whose eyes seem a bit unfocused.

Hazel has other photographs of Aston. In this he is a young man with wavy black hair and a moustache. He is wearing a high collar and a suit with a vest. This was how he must have looked at the beginning of his career as a lawyer and a sportsman . . . for he was that too. His obituary in the *Daily Gleaner* said that in his youth he had been "enthusiastic on cycle racing," a member of the Royal Jamaica Yacht Club, and a crack rifle shot. I remember the Yacht Club . . . there were wood shavings and a smell of paint. He kept a boat there, a runabout with an outboard motor. He still played tennis and went on bird shooting expeditions in the country.

The obituary said, also, that as a young man he was interested in literature and took part in debates. Something must have changed him . . . I never saw him read anything but a law book or journal and the newspapers. He took a newspaper from England as well as the *Gleaner*.

In this photograph he is wearing the uniform of the Jamaica Reserve Regiment, with a slouch hat, the kind worn by horsemen in the Boer War. I suppose the Reserve Regiment would have been called to arms if the Boers or the Kaiser had come marching up King Street. But he wasn't a horseman . . . I think he would have disliked a horse. It wasn't as manageable as a bicycle or a boat.

He is wearing a holster. The revolver it conceals must be the Webley he kept in the bottom drawer of the desk in his study, that I used to peer at, the same that my brother Herbert pointed at the cook, for which he was flogged when his father came home.

❧

My brother was away at a boarding school in the country so I played alone. I went out in the yard and found the garden boy rolling the tennis court or watering flower beds. He was a good-natured fellow who had walked down from the country to find work. He went barefoot and cooked his lunch of dumplings or rice and peas in the yard, hanging a can on a wire over some sticks. I asked him to tell me a Nancy story. The stories featured not only Brer Nancy, the long-legged spider, but Brer Tiger, Brer Alligator, Brer Donkey, and Brer Crow. The garden boy lived in a small room behind the house . . . I saw inside it once. There was just a bed and a chair. The lives of servants were invisible: they came and went, told to go because they were lazy and impertinent. There would be a garden boy with a different name watering the flowers.

A man came once a week to give my mother singing lessons. I heard the sound of the piano and her voice rising . . . she sang the same notes over and over again. She had shown me a photograph of herself in costume, posing as Delilah, hands above her head with the palms turned out. Together we looked at *The Victor Book of the Opera*. There was a picture of a man wearing a sword and a hat with a big feather, and a woman in a long gown that swept the floor. She was a princess; you could see this because she was wearing a crown. It was called a tiara.

There were pictures of opera houses in Berlin, Milan, and San Francisco. They had balconies, rows of seats, lights that hung in clusters called chandeliers.

A woman stood with her hands on her ships and a cigarette in her mouth. Another was dancing by herself. It was "The Shadow Dance."

She wound the gramophone and put on a record. Bells chimed

and voices struck up a song. She had a faraway look on her face. I thought how wonderful it must be to live where people sang instead of talking, among such scenes . . . a canal in Venice, a bazaar, a forest clearing. She showed me the picture of a woman with a pointed hat and earrings that hung to her shoulders. She was wearing little above the waist, her belly button clearly visible. A long skirt like a curtain covered the rest, falling to the floor. She had dark eyes . . . I thought she looked like my mother. "Pons," she read, "as Lakmé."

At the end of our lane was South Camp where the British soldiers were barracked. The breeze that made the leaves rustle brought the notes of bugle calls. When a new regiment came to the island we would go to see them march in with their tropical shorts, sun helmets, and rifles. When I came home I would line up my troops on the floor. They were the shotgun shells my father brought home from his bird-shooting. The Remingtons with their brass were like the cuirassiers at Waterloo. I had a cannon he made for me out of a section of pipe. It was powered by rubber bands. You pulled the bolt back till it clicked, aimed, and pulled the trigger, and the projectile went flying through the ranks of charging Frenchmen.

In the afternoon a breeze came from the sea, rustling the vine on the veranda. Tea was served there at four . . . the governess saw to it that I was washed and scrubbed behind the ears and put into clean clothes. We sat on the veranda and the maid in her white apron brought the tray. Sometimes we had a guest, one of the English ladies my mother had met at the Liguanea Club where she played golf. Or it would be my father's sister, Aunt May, of whom Rosalind was fond. She poured tea into the cups.

May had changed since the family photograph was taken. Then she had been a young woman . . . now she was a woman in her fifties who had not married. She lived with her sister Edith who was married to the Postmaster General. When our mother traveled to New York to visit her family Aunt May came to take care of the household.

The day of our mother's sailing was filled with emotion. We

drove to the dock to see her off. There were smells of coffee and pimento. We walked up the gangplank onto the deck and down stairs and through a corridor where fans were going. There was a smell of the sea. The cabin was small and her trunk seemed to take up half of it. My father lifted me up to look through the porthole.

The ship's horn boomed and made everyone jump. She began to cry. "Now Rosalind," he said. Then we were on the dock, watching the white steamer pull out and turn. It grew smaller, making for the mouth of the harbor at Port Royal. Then it was gone.

When she returned, as in a movie played backward everything happened in reverse. The steamer appeared and grew large. She was waving from the rail. You were all together in the car coming home. The trunk was being unpacked. There was a "Marx" tractor for you. You put books on the floor and the tractor climbed over them and kept going.

It was after one of her voyages to New York that the trouble began. She and my father could be heard quarreling . . . she was crying, I put my hands over my ears and went out in the yard.

Then, one day, she disappeared. No one told me why. They said she had gone away . . . that was all. This was the great blow of my life, and it occurred in silence. I did not shed a tear . . . the thing was overwhelming. There is no way for a child to know that the grief he feels is not the whole of life but only a part of it. This misery must be life . . . from the silence of those around me I took it to be so. It would have been wrong to complain.

I did not think of asking my father, who surely would have known why my mother was no longer with us. The matter-of-fact air he put on, going to his office and returning, implied that questions were uncalled-for, and neither my brother nor I was to ask them . . . that our mother's having gone away was none of our business.

I buried my anguish deep, and there it would remain, "A grief without a pang, vast, void, and drear." It would affect my life, especially my relations with women, but it harmed my imagination too, for you cannot suppress one part of feeling without suppressing others.

Coleridge has written on this subject. There is nothing psychology can tell us about the human mind that has not been said by a poet.

> For not to think of what I needs must feel,
>> But to be still and patient, all I can;
> And haply by abstruse research to steal
>> From my own nature all the natural man—
>> This was my sole resource, my only plan:
> Till that which suits a part infects the whole,
> And now is almost grown the habit of my soul.

I would see my mother again. One afternoon I went with my father to a house near the sea, at Bournemouth, that he was thinking of buying. It wasn't finished, it was littered with sawdust and wood. We were standing in the middle of an empty room when my mother appeared in the doorway. She was holding a revolver and pointing it at him. "Rosalind," he said, and walked across the room and took it from her hand. She fell to the floor and shrieked, frothing at the mouth.

The next meeting was not so dramatic. She was living in town and had a showplace where she sold cosmetics. I was taken to see her at her place of business. There were bottles on shelves . . . she unscrewed the top of one and showed me a yellow paste, and put a dab of it on the back of my hand. She said it was skin-nourishing cream.

There was no future in Jamaica for a woman who had left her husband. No lawyer would take her case—they were afraid of my father. She left the island and went to live in Toronto. My brother and I were to stay with our father's relatives, the Fletchers, and I was to go to school in Kingston.

"It was run by three sisters," Douglas tells me. He had gone before me to the same school. One sister taught mathematics, another geography, another music.

I tell him there was a tamarind tree in the schoolyard and he looks at me with surprise . . . so there was. How is it that one remembers a tamarind tree when so many things one would like to remember have dimmed? The fruit of the tamarind tree has a sweet but acid taste . . . it is tempting but it puts your teeth on edge.

In the evenings I would watch Douglas doing his homework. He drew figures with a pair of compasses and a protractor, studied Latin, or memorized lines of verse. He recited:

> Lars Prosena of Clusium
> > By the Nine Gods he swore
> That the great house of Tarquin
> > Should suffer wrong no more.

It was the first time I had heard poetry, except for nursery rhymes, and he made it sound exciting.

His sister Sybil worked at the public library. She wrote stories . . . about fairies, or about ladies and gentlemen who were in love. They were forced to part but they remained true to their memories. She urged me to write stories and I tried.

2

The Negril Beach Club
Tuesday, June 4

Two days ago we drove from Kingston to Munro, across the Liguanea plain then into the mountains. At Mandeville we stopped for tea and talked to the hotel owner, a Chinese woman who complained about politicians' messing with business. She said that life was pleasant in Mandeville: there was no crime, only break-ins.

We went down a mountain, along a valley, and up another mountain. I remembered when I was a boy returning to school how my heart sank with every mile that brought us closer to the red roofs on the crest of the mountain. "In arce sitam quis occultabit." And there they were. Who would have thought I would ever see them again!

The headmaster and his wife received us. The boys were assembling in the chapel. Douglas and I sat up front in the choir stalls, Miriam and Hazel at the back with the faculty. The English teacher introduced me and regretted the decline of interest in English at the school. One of the boys read my poem about the willows. It was an expression of pubescent sexuality, but in spite of the title, "Desire," no one seemed to have understood this.

I was called on to speak. I said that I was returning the book I had borrowed from a master, H. J. Andrews, fifty-one years ago—it had been on my conscience ever since. I said that at times they might think their lessons hard, but they should know that everything they learned now would be invaluable . . . it would enable them to do what they wanted . . . there was no limit to what they might accomplish.

Only afterwards did it occur to me that no matter how hard the boys studied their opportunities would be limited, for they were black. Munro used to be a private school. The boys came from everywhere and were of all colors and races—the history of Jamaica recapitulated in their names: Fonseca, Mendes, Fox, Cargill, MacNab, Bacquie, Lopez, Chin Sue. Munro was now a state school serving the parish of St. Elizabeth. Where there had been a hundred and forty boys, there were now more than seven hundred. But the buildings remained the same, and were deteriorating. The frame of a new building stood unfinished for lack of funds. I looked into my old dormitory. Where thirty beds had been, there were ninety, double-deckers ranged down the middle of the room as well as at the sides.

I walked around the grounds with Miriam. This was the Sixth Form where, as a small boy, I had the temerity to look in through the window. This was where the big boys were, and Weller called me in and made me run the gauntlet. They kicked me across the room and through the door, the last kick being Weller's, at the base of my spine as though he meant to break it.

I showed her Top Rock, and the willows where I used to lie and read Housman's poems and Hardy's novels. We stood at Long Wall looking down at the view I used to have every evening as I walked the barbecue: the mountain falling to a shelf with the football fields, then precipitously to a plain and the sea. It was here when I was a boy that I met the man who said he came from America and used to be a Munro boy. I have imagined that if I were to return to Munro and stand by the wall in the dusk I would meet the specter of my young self. But this meeting was not to be: the boys no longer walked up and down the barbecue. They couldn't, for the square had been converted into tennis courts and fenced off.

I am writing this on the patio adjoining our apartment at the Negril Beach Club. We are the guests of Doctor Kenneth McNeill and his wife Valerie, who own the hotel. They used to own more of the land hereabouts—they were pioneers of the tourist trade at Negril—but they ran short of funds and had to sell some of their acres. Ken McNeill no longer practices medicine—he is a member of Parliament and head of the Public Service, in charge of salaries and promotions.

Ken's father was a farmer and a politician. Ken went to Munro College. He had to leave school one year and go to the States for an operation. There were several operations . . . the disease and the cure left him partially crippled, he walks with a limp. When he came back to school my brother gave him exercises to build up his body and he learned to wrestle and box.

He was present in the gym, as I was, when the boxing team from Eton came to give an exhibition. Eton was the most famous public school in England and we thought our boys were taking an awful chance getting in the ring with Etonians. Our light-heavyweight, a rawboned fellow named Lynch, was matched with their light-heavy. The bell rang, one or two blows were exchanged, then the laws of nature seemed to have been suspended . . . the Etonian was lying on his back, out cold. Lynch hovered above him apologetically, then he and the sportsmaster carried him back to his corner.

This made us thoughtful. We had thought that English school-boys must be infinitely better at everything than we could ever hope to be. Apparently it was not so.

After leaving school Ken went to London and studied medicine at St. Bartholomew's Hospital. When war came he continued his studies in Cambridge, then he returned to London, but was unable to find a post . . . I suppose his being black had something to do with it. He told the hospital authorities that if he couldn't find a suitable position he would return to Jamaica, and they asked him if he would do plastic surgery. So he moved to Birmingham where he operated on burn wounds. After Normandy there were hundreds, for the Germans were using flame-throwing tanks. It was wonderful how the men survived massive burns . . . they were young and in top physical condition. He operated from nine in the morning to nine at night, then made rounds. He did four hundred skin grafts, beside reconstructing jaws and other parts of the body.

Ken McNeill is an extraordinary man and he hasn't let being black stand in his way. The author of *Self Help* would have been delighted with him. His success, however, isn't due entirely to his own efforts—his parents were able to provide him with a good education. The majority of Jamaicans aren't so fortunate.

Like the Rasta who talked to Miriam and Hazel at his roadside stand . . . He told them he had to stay up all night guarding his wares. He had a bunch of bananas but a thief came and stole it. "I can't progress, mon," he said.

✤

Ciboney
June 6

On this day, forty-seven years ago, G Company was moving inland from Utah Beach. We had seen our first dead, American as well as German. In a few hours we'd be digging in along the hedgerows.

And opening a box of K-rations. There was a can of meat, two biscuits, a bar of chocolate that tasted like clay, powdered coffee, sugar, and cigarettes of a brand none of us had ever seen.

Today for lunch I had seafood fritters, curried seafood, a slice of layer cake, white wine, and Jamaican coffee. Miriam had the seafood fritters and a salad consisting of pasta, chicken, tomato, olives, and a mustard vinaigrette sauce.

We are the guests of Peter and Beverly Rousseau at the complex of villas called Ciboney, sharing a suite with Douglas and Hazel. The villa is luxurious: two suites with large bathrooms, a living room, and a pool.

We have grown fond of Douglas and Hazel. We have been traveling together for days and have got along very well. We had one memorable adventure when the car hit a pothole and two of the tires went flat. Douglas hitched a ride to the nearest village and came back with a tire. There were two men on bicycles: one was transporting the tire, the other Douglas perched sideways on the crossbar. The ambassador was grinning . . . he looked about ten years old.

Douglas and Hazel have been married for fifty years. Her relatives weren't too pleased when she married him, for she is white and he is colored. In 1968 there were demonstrations, and some men in the crowd, hooligans she calls them, threw stones at cars being driven by white people. They saw her driving by and came running towards her, shouting, "Dere wan a dem now!" They threw stones and she was terribly frightened.

When she went to the United States she was required to fill out a form that had a place for you to state your race. If you came from the West Indies you were to state that you were black.

The road back to Kingston was blocked at Bog Walk by the recent rains, so we made a detour over a mountain road with potholes every few yards. The line of cars and trucks was moving slowly, then it stopped. A car came down the road as though fleeing from a disaster, the driver shouting, "Turn back!" Another car came by. As it slowed to pass Douglas called to the driver, "What's happening?" This fellow was more cheerful. "Give it a try, mon," he said.

People were getting out of their cars and walking up to the turn in the road. Douglas and I joined them. They were saying that a tractor trailer had jackknifed at the turn. If this were true we would be stuck here, for there was a precipice on one side of the road and a hill on the other. You couldn't turn around.

A man in army uniform appeared at the turn. He was shouting and the people who had gone up to see were coming back. We turned around too. In a few minutes an army truck came down the road, then the line of traffic began to move. When we got to the turn soldiers were directing traffic. Where was the tractor trailer that had jackknifed and blocked the road? At the bottom of the valley perhaps.

So we made it back to Kingston and lunch. I am sitting on the veranda at the Fletchers' instead of by the road with a biscuit and a bottle of Scotch.

A mongoose just ran across a corner of the veranda. Hazel says there are two, Herman and Hilda, and sometimes one goes by followed by three little mongooses.

From two to five a blanket of heat covers Kingston and nothing moves . . . except mosquitoes. Half a dozen arrive droning and attack your ankles and the back of your neck from every angle. They are so slight as to be almost invisible, and so quick that you can't hit them. Mosquito repellent is the only defense until it wears off. Or you may retire to a bedroom and turn on the air-conditioning—mosquitoes hate the cold. A mosquito net will keep them out, but I dislike sleeping under a net.

At five there's a breath of wind. Two ground doves light on the grass and walk around like priests, looking at their feet. A black dog crosses the grass beyond the veranda, followed by a brown dog. They are thin and famished, as all animals seem to be in Jamaica.

Yesterday Miriam and I went downtown with Douglas to see his office. The law firm of Myers, Fletcher and Gordon occupies a building with several floors. The office looks very up-to-date with electronic equipment and paintings and pieces of sculpture. There were one or two pieces by Edna Manley I thought I recognized. The young writers of *Public Opinion* used to meet at her house. She was interested in what young people thought.

On the way back we drove up King Street to the park, passing the statue of Norman Manley, Edna's husband. He and my father worked together on cases. Douglas tells me that people used to say that to have Manley on your side in a case was to be ninety per cent sure of winning. To have Aston Simpson prepare your brief and Norman Manley argue it was to be a hundred per cent sure.

Manley became the First Premier of the Jamaican government. His statue showed him standing with feet apart, one arm across his breast, the other extended at his side grasping a scroll. I supposed it was the constitution of Jamaica, written following the Independence he did so much to obtain, and he was defying those who would take it from him.

To the right was Coke Church where the Fletchers used to go on Sunday and I had to go too. Then the Ward Theatre. When I was a little boy I was taken there to see the magician. He called a little girl in a party frock to come up to the stage. Then he called me. He told me to walk over and introduce myself to her, and to push out my chest, but I stuck out my stomach instead and everyone laughed.

Last night we went to a party in the hills above Kingston. At night you see clusters of light in the hills. Each has a name: Mona, Ravina, Charlmont, Billy Dunn . . . Present were three Jamaican poets we've met, Ralph Thompson, Edward Baugh, and Mervyn Morris, and a novelist, John Hearne. I talked about my idea of having one or two young Americans come to teach at Munro. And an American college might be persuaded to give scholarships to Munro boys, an American equivalent of the Rhodes scholarship. Jamaicans used to look to England for a university education, but the island is now in the American orbit. Thousands of American tourists come to Jamaica every year, but no one, Jamaican or American, seems to have thought about the opportunities in education.

My other idea is to establish a connection between the University of the West Indies and a university in the States. Exchanges of faculty could be worked out, an American coming to Jamaica to teach American literature, for example, a Jamaican going to the States to teach the literature of the Caribbean.

They listened politely. Eddie Baugh said that the thing to do was persuade some high-level administrator in the States to come to Jamaica and see for himself. And this is what I shall try to do. I have no talent for administration—I can only put those who administrate in touch with one another.

Hazel is having some upholstering done. She says that he is a good upholsterer but for months no one has been able to find him. He probably has woman trouble, a second family somewhere, maybe a third, and is hiding out.

Jamaicans, with exceptions such as my cousin and his wife, take marriage lightly. Many have children out of wedlock.

Recently an American politician who was thinking of running for president was discovered to have spent a night with a woman not his wife. The ensuing publicity compelled him to withdraw. In Jamaica, Douglas says, it would probably have got him elected.

My father's adultery destroyed his marriage and left his children poor. Our stepmother may have assured him that she would take care of us, so there was no need to make provision for us in his will. He may just have been foolish enough to believe her.

I am not inclined to blame him for I loved him dearly. Had he lived we would have fallen out, for he would have wanted me to be a lawyer and I would have wanted to write poems and see the world. When the war came I would have gone to it, and after that I would have done what I wanted. So it would have come to the same in the end.

I had dreamed of going back. In the dream I was walking by the sea and drawing near my father's house with a feeling of excitement. And there it was, but the bright colors of walls and roof, white and red, had faded. It looked gloomy and deserted.

Going back was like being in a dream. I came with Miriam and Douglas, driving on the street I used to walk alone when I returned from the library in Kingston or a movie. It was as though the area had been struck by a blight. The houses had broken windows and hadn't been painted in years . . . the gardens were patches of dirt overrun with weeds. The street went down to the sea and Bournemouth Bath where we went swimming on Sunday with our parents. After swimming we would sit by the balcony that overlooked the pool and watch the people splashing and pushing each other off the raft and shrieking. The loudspeaker played dance music and my brother and I had a Delaware Punch.

When our father married again he bought a house only a short walk from Bournemouth. I would go swimming with Dennis Anderson or go by myself and sit by the pool and read. Now the fence was down and the pool lay open to the street, a white cavity glaring in the sun.

There was our gate, next to the place where the drowned man lay. It was after a hurricane . . . a flash flood came rushing down the gully. The body was covered with a sheet of zinc but the bare feet stuck out. The body left a hollow in the ground. When I came home at night lamplight glimmered in the hollow.

There had been an empty lot between our house and the Andersons', the last house on the block. Now it was occupied by a factory or warehouse. The concrete walls had cracked—the building had gone through a cycle of use and been abandoned. All since I stood here last.

To the right of the drive there used to be a separate building, the "carpenter's shop" where my father spent hours on weekends sawing, drilling, hammering, using a blowtorch. The building had vanished. Where it stood there was a patch of concrete on the earth as though giant claws had wrenched the building from its foundation and flown away with it.

They say that if you return to a house where you lived when

you were young it seems smaller, but this was large, larger than the house in my dream. Facing us was the veranda. The bedrooms and my father's study were on the second floor . . . at the other end of the house was the room I shared with my brother. He sat there at night . . . he was supposed to be studying law, but he was reading *How to Make Friends and Influence People* and underlining significant passages. Or this month's issue of *Physical Culture*. The red tiles of the roof had fallen and been replaced with sheets of zinc. The windows were empty frames . . . a black woman stood in one, looking down at us. A squatter, Douglas remarked. He called to her: "We want to have a look round. All right?" She said nothing but stood staring. Had we come to put her out?

The veranda was where I had my trains. The Bassett-Lowke tank engine pulled its coaches around the track, passing the station, running through a tunnel and over a bridge. The next time it came around I tripped the clockwork motor and brought the train to a stop at the station. There were people: a man in a business suit, a station master holding up a flag, a porter pushing a handcart with baggage, and a mother waving good-bye to her son. The train started again and went around. The man in the business suit, the station master, the porter and the mother remained in the same positions. The train came by again and did not stop.

We walked around to the other side of the house. The ground was littered with rubbish, fragments of rusting iron, turds. A man was squatting on his hams. He was black, with Rastafarian dreadlocks. But dreadlocks are worn by many Jamaicans, they have no special significance. A child, a boy of ten or so, was standing by him. The man looked at us and down again . . . he was doing something, scraping or cutting. The child left his side and followed us.

My father's bedroom opened on a porch. There he kept a telescope on a tripod with which he swept the harbor. The porch was no longer open to sky and sea; it had been enclosed with shutters. At the other end of the house there used to be an outside staircase by which my brother and I could come and go . . . this, like the carpenter's shop, had been torn away, and the door at the top boarded up. The second floor had the appearance of a fortress.

I remembered something my brother told me. Our stepmother had two children: a girl who was three or four years old when we left, and a boy born shortly before our father's death. One night a robber entered the house by the outside staircase and beat up the boy. Our stepmother had the staircase removed, but there was a second break-in, after which she left the house and moved to the country.

There had been a lawn going down from the house to the sea. Soon after buying the house my father built a motorboat, that is, he put one together. He obtained a ship's lifeboat, installed an engine, and put a roof over the whole except for a short deck at the bow and a couple of feet at the stern. It looked like an old woman wearing a bonnet. He christened it "The Seahawk." Our stepmother, after a trip or two, refused to go. We would travel across the harbor to Port Royal and back. If a ship were anchored in the harbor he would circle it slowly.

Now and then it would be a warship. The sailors came to Bournemouth, men with very white skin. They shouted and ran along the sides of the pool, and pushed each other in. They were poor swimmers. They climbed on the diving tower, held their noses, and jumped. There were rings suspended from a rope above the pool, from one side to the other. You were supposed to swing hand over hand across the pool. The sailors would get halfway across, hang for a while, and drop.

The ground between the house and shore was overgrown with bushes so that I could just see the water and some posts sticking up like broken teeth, all that remained of the dock.

Heine has a poem about a pine and a palm:

> Ein Fichtenbaum steht einsam
> Im Norden auf kahler Höh.

Ihn schlafert; mit weisser Decke
Umhullen ihn Eis und Schnee.

The pine sleeps on a desolate height in the north, covered with ice
and snow. It is dreaming of a palm tree far away in the tropics
that stands on a burning cliff and grieves in silence and solitude.
At times I have felt like that pine. Living in North America I
would think of the tropics, of bicycling in quiet lanes or lying by
a pool reading *Typhoon*.

The land where I grew up, my "Morgenland," no longer exists;
the lanes and the pool have vanished. The boys I went to school
with have been scattered about the world. The empire on which,
it was said, the sun never set, has vanished. The citizens of that
empire felt secure. They believed that their way of life, traditions
and laws, would be passed on through the generations. That the
British empire would vanish within a generation was as unthink-
able as that the sun and moon would change places.

I do not regret the passing of the old colonial dispensation. It
was built on an assumption of racial superiority. To be told so still
surprises some Englishmen, especially those who never lived in a
British colony. When I lived in England I was assured on several
occasions that the English had no race prejudice—Americans
might be prejudiced but not the English. This kind of thing is
what people mean when they speak of the hypocrisy of the
English. It isn't hypocrisy but a staggering complacency: their
sense of racial superiority enables them to think well of themselves no matter what they do.

I left Jamaica when I was seventeen and emigrated to the
United States. Instead of going to Oxford I went to Columbia.
There followed three years in the American army. After this I no
longer thought of myself as a Jamaican, and my writing changed.
As time passed it would change radically, so that I was regarded
as an American, not a Jamaican, poet.

When I was a boy, Europe presented a face like that which
Prospero showed to Caliban at first: it was wise and just, and the
voice in which it spoke was magic. The possessor of that voice was

able to conjure up spirits to do his bidding. How could I not love him? But when I became a man this voice threatened to stifle my own. It was the voice of a ruling class, heard on the docks and in railway stations ordering the natives about.

It has taken me a lifetime to forget that voice and hear the sound of my own.

⚘

Working Late

A light is on in my father's study.
"Still up?" he says, and we are silent,
looking at the harbor lights,
listening to the surf
and the creak of coconut boughs.

He is working late on cases.
No impassioned speech! He argues from evidence,
actually pacing out and measuring,
while the fans revolving on the ceiling
winnow the true from the false.

Once he passed a brass curtain rod
through a head made out of plaster
and showed the jury the angle of fire—
where the murderer must have stood.
For years, all through my childhood,
if I opened a closet . . . bang!
There would be the dead man's head
with a black hole in the forehead.

All the arguing in the world
will not stay the moon.
She has come all the way from Russia
to gaze for a while in a mango tree

and light the wall of a veranda,
before resuming her interrupted journey
beyond the harbor and the lighthouse
at Port Royal, turning away
from land to the open sea.

Yet, nothing in nature changes, from that day to this,
she is still the mother of us all.
I can see the drifting offshore lights,
black posts where the pelicans brood.

And the light that used to shine
at night in my father's study
now shines as late in mine.

An End and
a Beginning

I have returned to my father's house—I want to see inside. One of the squatters, a woman, is looking down from the window of his bedroom. I speak to her, saying that I would like to look around . . . I used to live here. She is not the forbidding woman of my first visit—this one has a pleasant face. I am carrying a camera and she asks if I want to take pictures. I say that I do and she says, "No problem."

They have put up a zinc fence on the far side of the veranda, screening it from the shore. The veranda is being used as a bed-room—a man is sitting on some bedding in a corner.

I walk down to the water and take pictures of the house through the bushes that have grown up. I photograph the broken piles where my father's boat, "The Seahawk," used to be moored.

A man is walking towards me. He is young, in his twenties. He asks, "Are you the owner?" I tell him no, but I used to live here as a boy, I grew up here. He says his name is Rohan Moore and he is a painter, an artist. I tell him I am a writer and we shake hands.

We walk back to the house together and he invites me in. It is eleven o'clock and the sun is shining brightly but the house is dark. We go up the staircase. The railing is rough to my hand, it hasn't been painted in years. There is no carpeting underfoot, only bare boards, and the wall is unpainted.

We go into my father's bedroom. It is cluttered with furniture, not just a bedroom but living quarters for a family. The woman who was standing in the window is absent, but two children are walking about and there is an infant sleeping in a crib face down. Rohan says that the children are Stepheny, a girl, and Brandon, a boy. They are his girlfriend's children by the man she used to be with. The baby in the crib is his . . . his name is Shango.

There is a large bureau. A television set is standing on it and also a stereo. Why did I think that squatters wouldn't want possessions? They want a house and everything that goes with it. It doesn't have to be theirs.

Where my father's bed used to be, where he used to sleep with my stepmother, there is an empty space. Against the white sheets he looks darker than usual and somewhat smaller. The night table holds a spoon in a glass and bottles of medicine. He looks at me through his glasses. "Did Mims give you your pocket money?"

I say that she did.

"Well then, everything seems to be in order." He pauses, then he says, "I don't want you to worry. Whatever happens you'll be well taken care of."

Rohan is calling me to come and look at his paintings. He is out on the porch. It used to be open to sky and sea, and my father used to sit there. He had a telescope on a tripod and would look at the harbor. The porch has been enclosed with shutters and is dark like the rest of the house. It serves as another room.

Rohan's paintings are stacked against a wall. He lifts one out, "The Banana Man." It isn't finished, he says, he is still working on the frame. Pins have been stuck into the frame all around, half an inch apart. Apparently his idea of painting, like Gauguin's, includes the frame.

He had a visit yesterday by a woman who said that he had considerable talent and he shouldn't let anyone tell him what to do but follow his own way of painting. He shows me a snapshot of herself the visitor gave him: a white woman, young and pretty. She lives in Paris and says she can sell his paintings there.

He talks about himself. He grew up in this neighborhood, a few streets away. He is twenty-three. He wants to do what he likes, not what people think he should.

He shows me his paint box, the flat metal case with water colors one gives to a child. He says it cost two hundred dollars. That would be eight American. All the paints have been used up. I take out my wallet and give him the money for a new box. He thanks me. Maybe he was hoping I'd give him the money, maybe not . . . in any case it would have been only natural. I am rich compared to him.

There is a room I want to see, the one at the other end of the house where I lived with my brother. But the door is locked and the people are away. That's just as well: there is always a room you aren't meant to see.

We go downstairs and Rohan introduces me to a man who says that he's a song writer, he writes "song and sing-song." His name is Linton Williamson but he calls himself Bobby Soul. I give him my ballpoint and tell him that I hope he'll write a song with it.

I want a stone from the sea to place on my father's grave. I walk down to the shore with Rohan. I find a stone and he hands me another.

We walk to the gate where I left the car. My driver is sitting in it, he hasn't moved. He lives downstairs in my cousin Douglas's house as caretaker and drives a taxi on the side. Why did I ask him to drive me to a slum, and go nosing about an old house, talking to these people?

Bobby Soul joins us. People have come out of the house and are watching us. They must be everywhere in the house, not just the bedrooms but the drawing room and dining room, pantry and kitchen.

I'm glad you're living here, I tell Rohan and Bobby Soul. When we were here it wasn't a happy place.

They say I can come and live here any time.

✤

The graveyard is littered and headstones have been overturned and broken. Goats are running about, leaping from one grave to another. An elderly, bearded goat sits on a tomb with his family around him. On another there is a ragged man with long hair. He is lying on his back. As I approach he raises himself on an elbow and stares at me.

I walk among the graves looking for my father's. In one place the earth has fallen, a malodorous pit six feet deep. Among the ranked headstones my eye is caught by one of shining white marble. It holds his name, the dates of his birth and death, and some lines of verse saying that he bade farewell to glory in exchange for life eternal. My stepmother must have found this in a book of epitaphs for all occasions—it bears no relation to the man.

He was a lawyer and he loved his work. He liked his "carpenter's shop" and cruising the harbor on Sunday in his boat. He wouldn't have cared for life eternal: it would have been like the Sabbaths of his childhood when you had to go to church and weren't allowed to play.

When I was a young man I worked for a publishing house in New York. One day the editor-in-chief came by my desk and deposited a pile of magazines titled *Tomorrow* and asked me to look through them for "book ideas." I picked one up at random and leafed through it . . . articles about the occult, dreams, weird coincidences, far-fetched events that happened to be true. I picked up another and read a paragraph here and there. I couldn't see what earthly use any of this could be to us: the house had a reputation for dignified publishing . . . books that were well written and rather dull. Though we published novels our bestseller was a cookbook. I picked up another copy of *Tomorrow*.

There was an article by a woman with the title of countess before her name. She had lived in Jamaica as a young girl. One night she had a dream in which a friend named Aston appeared. In the morning she told her mother about it and said that Aston must be coming to visit. Her mother pooh-poohed the idea, for he lived a considerable distance away. But that same day he appeared, being driven in a buggy to Kingston to begin the study of law.

The young man in the buggy was my father. He turns his face toward me and his eyes meet mine. He looks away and the contact is broken. He has his life and I have mine.